POWER TOOLS

Other Books by the Authors

Smart Moves: 140 Checklists to Bring Out the Best from You and Your Team

Smart Moves for People in Charge: 130 Checklists to Help You Be a Better Leader

Yes, You Can! 1,200 Inspiring Ideas for Work, Home, and Happiness

What to Say to Get What You Want: Strong Words for 44 Challenging Bosses, Employees, Coworkers, and Customers

What to Ask When You Don't Know What to Say: 555 Powerful Questions to Use for Getting Your Way at Work

COMEX: The Communication Experience in Human Relations

Speaking Skills for Bankers

By Sam Deep

Human Relations in Management

A Program of Exercises for Management and Organizational Behavior
(with James A. Vaughan)

Introduction to Business: A Systems Approach
(with William D. Brinkloe)

Studies in Organizational Psychology
(with Bernard M. Bass)

Current Perspectives for Managing Organizations
(with Bernard M. Bass)

By Lyle Sussman

Communications for Supervisors and Managers

Increasing Supervisory Effectiveness

Power Tools

33 *Management Inventions You Can Use Today*

SAM DEEP · LYLE SUSSMAN

Addison-Wesley
Reading, Massachusetts

Many of the designations used by manufacturers and sellers to distinguish their products are claimed as trademarks. Where those designations appear in this book and Addison-Wesley was aware of a trademark claim, the designations have been printed in initial capital letters (e.g., Post-it).

Library of Congress Cataloging-in-Publication Data

Deep, Samuel D.

Power tools : thirty-three management inventions you can use today / Sam Deep, Lyle Sussman.

p. cm.

Includes index.

ISBN 0-201-77297-3

1. Management—Handbooks, manuals. I. Sussman, Lyle, 1944- II. Title.

HD31.D4214 1997

658—DC21 97–39809

CIP

Addison-Wesley is an imprint of Addison Wesley Longman, Inc.

Cover design by Suzanne Heiser
Text design by Diane Levy
Set in 11.5-point Walbaum by GAC/Shepard Poorman

1 2 3 4 5 6 7 8 9-DOH-0201009998
First printing, December 1997

Contents

Introduction

We've been on quite a benchmarking journey, and we'd like to show you our snapshots.

Our recent speaking, training, and consulting adventures have taken us to companies from California to New York and from Florida to North Dakota.

We've seen the insides of both complex conglomerates and less complicated mom-and-pop shops. We've met some incredibly inventive managers and others who could barely keep up. We've basked in warm sunshine in plant buildings that had no windows, and we've needed flashlights to find our way around dismal offices even though their walls were of glass.

In these diverse settings we've taught and we've learned. This book is a record of that teaching and that learning. It is a carefully crafted collection of 33 practical, powerful, and precise management tools we either used or discovered in the process of helping pressured managers meet dozens of leadership challenges. Some of these devices have at their heart a planning tool; others grow out of diagnostic instruments; still others emerge from proven-to-be-effective management strategies.

Roughly a third of the tools are old standbys from our consulting arsenal that seem to be getting even better with age and more effective with use. You may have seen a few of these before, but perhaps not presented as usefully as firsthand experience with them now permits. Another third of the tools were created on the fly as we unearthed problems and challenges we'd never confronted before. We were thrilled at how well these new methods worked in the field. The final third of the book is inspired by terrific ideas that resourceful managers shared with us. The ones that made it into the book are the best of the "best practices" that we unearthed. We're especially excited by the opportunity to share with you these remarkable inventions by your colleagues.

You can get the same value from the Power Tools that others are receiving. First, study Chapter 1 to understand the five overriding management challenges that the tools prepare you to meet.

Second, use Chapter 2 to learn how the tools work. Chapter 2 is the owner's manual for the tools.

Your rush to dig into the tools may tempt you to skim or even to skip over Chapters 1 and 2. If so, at least slow down long enough to read the Action Index. It will direct you to the exact tools you need to solve the precise management problems you face. (Actually, we think of these dilemmas as being opportunities in disguise. We're convinced you'll agree after you see how the Power Tools transform these challenges into advantages for you and your team.)

Doctors keep their instruments handy, and so should you. Although these tools are printed on 200 pages of paper bound between two covers, they're not intended to be forgotten on a bookshelf. Keep them out where you can use them. They'll make your job easier. They'll make work more fulfilling for your team. Most important, they'll help you improve the bottom line.

Sam Deep
Lyle Sussman

POWER TOOLS

1 THE FIVE MANAGEMENT CHALLENGES: WHAT NEEDS TO BE FIXED AND WHY

You've heard the story.

A baffled home owner, unable to get water from any of his faucets, tries in vain to fix the problem himself. After scraping his knuckles, chipping tile, and screaming at his kids, he finally calls a plumber, even though he knows he'll pay dearly. The plumber arrives, checks out the faucets, and asks to see the main water line in the basement.

The plumber examines the line for a few minutes, runs his hand across a two-foot section, and removes a rubber mallet from his tool box. He strikes the line with a single no-nonsense blow. With one smack the water flows.

Before he leaves he writes up his invoice: "Fixed clogged water pipe: $75.00."

The homeowner is furious. "This is highway robbery. All you did was hit a pipe. I could have done that."

"True," says the plumber. "But you didn't. And if you had you might have busted the pipe."

The homeowner demands an itemized invoice. So the plumber writes the following:

Unclogging of Water Pipe: Itemized Charges	
Transporting self and tools to homeowner	$12.00
Choosing the tool to hit the pipe	12.00
Knowing where and how to hit the pipe	50.00
Hitting pipe	1.00
TOTAL	$75.00

The moral of the story? Anyone can hit a pipe. But a professional who truly understands the problem selects the right tool to hit the pipe, and knows where and how to hit it.

In the same way, any manager can attack a problem. It takes thoughtful and experienced managers to know *which* problems to attack, *when* to take them on, *where* to apply the pressure, and *how* to wage the campaign. And perhaps most important, they must use the *right* tool to solve the problem. To make sure that you solve the right problem with the right tool we have specifically designed your Power Tools to solve the most vexing problems confronting you and your organization: people problems.

Managers maintain people, not pipes. They need to be more delicate than plumbers as they respond to the difficulties they encounter. A bruised ego is more harmful than a bruised pipe. Mounting pressure is more damaging to a work team than to a control valve. Reduced productivity is far more costly than a blocked water flow.

Problems the Power Tools Solve: Five Management Challenges

In the next chapter you'll learn how to use the Power Tools to solve the toughest leadership and communication problems you face. This chapter is about those problems—64 of them in all—that make you need the tools.

Why so many problems? As the third millennium approaches, traumatic forces buffet you and your company. Thanks to earth-shaking transformations in technology, demographics, cultural values, economics, competition, and government regulations, you're managing in both the best of times and the worst of times. You're called on to confront challenges and exploit opportunities that yesterday's managers would not have imagined in their wildest dreams (or nightmares).

Sixty-four problems appear in the Action Index beginning on page 227. These are the ones we hear about over and over again from managers. They afflict all types of organizations and are as destructive to mom-and-pop shops as they are to complex conglomerates. They affect every type managerial function, doing as much damage to marketing managers as to financial officers. They cross international boundaries, being as prevalent in your plant on the Yucatan Peninsula as in your operation on Long Island. For the most part, they even transcend hierarchy, causing as much pain for CEOs as for first-line supervisors.

To understand the full impact of the problems solved by the tools in this book, you'll find it helpful to see that they are responses to five principal management challenges.

1. The Leadership Challenge

Let's set the record straight: management and leadership are not synonymous. We don't have a management challenge; we have a

Leadership Challenge. Corporations, schools, hospitals, governments, and armies have no trouble filling management slots, but they do have trouble filling leadership positions. Executive development programs don't have trouble teaching management skills; they do have trouble teaching leadership skills. To realize your dream of becoming CEO of a *Fortune* 100 company, don't hire a management coach; hire a leadership coach. Today's workforce does not want for competent managers; it hungers for inspiring leaders.

The difference between managers and leaders is not so much in what they achieve as in how they achieve it. While both a manager and a leader might achieve the same goal, they will achieve it in different ways.

- Managers motivate with sticks and carrots; leaders motivate through ownership and inspiration.
- Managers focus on goals and schedules; leaders focus on vision and values.
- Managers reduce cost and minimize waste; leaders produce new ideas and maximize energy.
- Managers focus on doing the thing right; leaders focus on doing the right thing.
- Managers leave a legacy measured in profitability and customer satisfaction; leaders add to that same legacy employee growth and satisfaction.

These differences between managers and leaders help to explain the major deficiencies in companies with a leadership void. The most common problems associated with impotent leadership are:

1. Employees who work with their hands and their heads, but not necessarily with their hearts and their souls
2. Activities fueled by projects and deadlines, rather than by dreams and vision
3. Employees acting as exploited hired hands, rather than as partners in a common cause

These three negative outcomes spawn nine of the problems listed in the Action Index. They result when the manager in you overrides the leader in you.

2. The Teamwork Challenge

In 1985 a group of recording artists gathered in a studio to record a song that eventually sold millions of copies worldwide. Even though each of the artists was famous enough to command top dollar, all royalties for "We Are the World" went for famine relief in Africa.

These singers were star soloists, unaccustomed to sharing microphones, stages, or adoration from their fans. Yet they became team players for a cause more compelling than individual gain. Lionel Ritchie, one of the performers, set the tone for teamwork among them in a simple and direct way. He placed a sign above the entrance to the studio door that read: "Check Your Ego at the Door."

In an effort to realize the full potential of their workforces, companies are asking employees to check their egos at the door. A hope for new levels of achievement is being entrusted to employee task forces, quality circles, project groups, empowered work crews, and self-directed teams. The intent is to tap into the power of synergy. True leaders realize that brilliant talent is meaningless unless the people who have that talent are molded into a unified force. This is the Teamwork Challenge.

That's the good news. The bad news is that in many companies teamwork is more of a hollow platitude or an elusive dream than a present reality. Just as there are problems associated with the Leadership Challenge, so too are there dilemmas for managers who take on the Teamwork Challenge. In fact, we've heard all too often the 14 complaints by managers who are trying to convert team play from fantasy into fact. These complaints appear in the Action Index.

3. The Motivation Challenge

Chances are good that you can identify with one of these four statements:

1. My employees don't feel enough ownership of the goals or the strategy of this enterprise.
2. Not enough people are following my lead.
3. Too many people around here don't have the same priorities I do.
4. How can I get my employees to *want* to do what they *have* to do?

These are just four of the 17 problems that cluster under the motivation rubic.

If you feel buried by the Motivation Challenge, you may be tempted to conclude that every employee who works for you is afflicted by an incurable malaise. Many discouraged managers would go even one step further to say that today's employee:

- Has an attitude problem
- Doesn't want to work hard
- Is looking for an excuse to file a worker's compensation claim
- Has the temper of a demented serial killer
- Is a chronic substance abuser
- Shirks responsibility
- Is waiting for the right opportunity to sue
- Can't wait to steal from you

Those who draw such conclusions are wrong. If you don't believe us, tell the employees at Saturn, Nordstrom, Netscape, Wal-Mart, Intel, Vencor, Res-Care, Disney, Hewlett Packard, and Microsoft that they have attitude problems and shirk responsibility. Tell these employees that they are trying to get as much money as they can for as little effort as possible. Tell them that they don't take pride in what they do. But make sure that before you say these things you plan your escape route.

Unfortunately, in too many companies this would be an accurate assessment of employee motivation. So often this description of alienated employees is right on the mark. But the accuracy of the description is less a result of employee attitudes than of manager behavior. Most managers *want* employees to feel ownership for the goals they set for them, but they just don't know how to do it. They *want* employees to be the most valuable asset on the balance sheet, but they just keep shooting themselves in the foot with unfortunate actions. Does this sound like you? Well, not for long, once you learn how to use the tools listed in the Action Index designed to help you meet the Motivation Challenge.

4. The Continuous Improvement Challenge

It's quite possible that on the day your grandfather retired, he had much the same skills and performed many of the same tasks as he did on the day he was hired. Contrast that stability with the degree and rate of change you experience on your job. If you perform the same tasks next year with the same technology you're using today, you are in a dead-end job, in a company about to go belly up, or in a dying industry. To respond to this environment of constant change, you must meet the Continuous Improvement Challenge.

In many respects the continuous improvement challenge is the inevitable consequence of the preceding three. As managers become leaders, as teamwork replaces individualism, and as employees are inspired to achieve ever-increasing levels of outcomes, everyone in the organization will be either planning for change, implementing change, or both. Learning, adapting, and transforming will become the norm, regardless of job description.

Your management lexicon contains a new vocabulary reflecting the Continuous Improvement Challenge: CQI (constant quality improvement), the Learning Organization (one that increases the intellectual capital of all its employees), Six Sigma Quality (improving processes and products to the point of zero defects), and Kaizen (Japanese for "continuous improvement"). Good enough just isn't good enough any more. The management guru Tom Peters puts it this way: "It's real simple. If we're not getting more, better, faster than they are getting more, better, faster, then we're getting less better or more worse."

Unfortunately, for every employee who thrives on continuous improvement there are many others who approach change as if they were attending a funeral. In the words of one anonymous pundit: the only person who likes change is a wet baby, and even that's debatable.

If getting employees excited about continuous improvement is difficult for you, you probably can't wait to see what tools have been created to meet this challenge. Go ahead and take a peek, but promise that you'll come right back to finish this chapter.

5. The Balance Challenge

In a management program we jointly conduct before large audiences, one of us stands at center stage and role-plays a CEO delivering a companywide announcement.

> *Folks, I have some bad news and some good news. First, the bad news. Because of increased competition and disastrous quarterly results we have to cut costs. Specifically, we are downsizing our staff by 15 percent. The good news is that because we'll have 15 percent fewer people, I'm reducing our expectations by 15 percent. So those of you who remain will be working with no more pressure and stress than before.*

Laughter? Of course. Imagine your boss telling you that, for whatever reason, goals have been scaled back. Fat chance! We live in a world of downsized staffs, upsized goals, and overstocked medicine cabinets.

The 13 problem statements in the Action Index for Your Balance Challenge can be summarized in one statement: I'm being forced to choose between increased market share and a full life. Rex Lee, president of Brigham Young University, captured the essence of these problems: "When I ask my doctors what kinds of things to avoid, their answer sounds like my job description." One of our clients, the owner of a small manufacturing company, concurs. He jestingly suggested expanding the offerings in the company vending machines to include Valium and Prozac.

In the "Work and Family" column published by *The Wall Street Journal,* Sue Shellenbarger reported the results of an informal survey of corporate recruiters. Her conclusion has significant implications for all companies competing for talent: "Questions about work-life balance—which in the past were saved for the final round of interviews, or never asked at all—are surfacing in job candidates' first round talks with employers."

Juan, Chen, and Mary will not tolerate what Tom, Dick, and Harry found acceptable. The "organization man" of the 1950s who was willing to sacrifice family for career has turned into the "total person" of the twenty-first century who wants not only a career but a rewarding personal life as well. The best and the brightest will not be attracted to, nor remain with, companies that fail to provide quality-of-work-life initiatives. Unless the corporate treadmill is in a company-sponsored exercise facility, employees may not get on it.

For the sake of both you and your employees, you must find a way to meet this fifth challenge. The Power Tools won't give you exercise machines or Valium, but they do offer strategies to bring sanity and balance back into life and work.

Now that you have some idea of the pipes you'll be hitting, it's time to turn your attention to the hammers themselves. The Power Tools' operation is completely described in Chapter 2. Read it thoroughly so that when you start to take the Power Tools—and they *are* powerful tools—out of their boxes you'll know exactly how to use them to exert the maximum leverage without hurting anyone or anything.

2 YOUR NEW POWER TOOLS: AN OWNER'S GUIDE

Now that you know what needs to be fixed and why, it's time to open your toolbox. But before you start smoothing, loosening, sharpening, tightening, probing, and connecting, you need to learn something about the tools themselves. This chapter answers two questions:

1. Why these particular tools?
2. How do you use them?

Why These Tools?

The comedian Tim Allen has built his reputation playing off the stereotype that a "real" man has lots of tools and is always looking to expand his toolbox. But the humor of his television program, *Home Improvement*, carries a broader message to managers of both genders. As your assignments become more complex you do need to acquire more tools.

A large toolbox generally signifies prestige and the potential to solve almost any problem that might occur. But plumbers, carpenters, and technicians aren't judged by the size of their toolboxes. Rather, they are judged by their ability to use the right tool for the right problem. Similarly, our goal is not to load you down with all the tools you *might* use, but rather to make available the most important ones you *will* use. Your toolbox (this book) is limited in its size by practical considerations, and so we had to be selective. To be included, a tool had to meet each of the following five criteria:

1. Each tool solves problems in at least one of the five challenge areas.

Nearly every tool listed in the Action Index (page 227) solves more than one problem within one of the five challenge areas. Several tools transcend challenges. For instance, *Culture Print* solves a total of nine problems in three of the five challenge areas.

2. Each tool leverages your most important resource: people.

The message of Chapter 1 was simple: the changing world has created five fundamental management challenges. All five of these challenges have a common theme: people. This book of Power Tools helps you solve the problems inherent whenever people join forces in modern corporations to meet ambitious goals. You solve these problems when you leverage the abilities, talents, and efforts of your people. That's what the selected tools do.

3. Each tool is designed for managers, not psychologists, trainers, or therapists.

Brooms, scissors, combs, screwdrivers, nails, rulers, doorbells, forks, and a multitude of other everyday tools make our lives easier, more fulfilling, and more productive. None of them comes with a 24-hour toll-free number or an instructional video. In the same way, most of the Power Tools are relatively easy to use even though they solve complex problems, have many component parts, and may initially look intimidating. A few are a bit formidable to pull off and may require some outside help, but the majority are do-it-yourselfers.

4. Each tool is problem-centered.

We often hear managers complain that training programs or management books contain interesting information but have little practical information that is relevant to their needs. You won't have this reaction to the Power Tools. Regardless of your job title, level of authority, company size, or industry, your new toolbox contains solutions to the problems you experience every day. Whether you're the manager of a small restaurant, the provost of a large university, or the head of a division in a multinational corporation, you are paid to get people to produce. Any manager reading this book who experiences the five challenges will discover relevant, practical, and timely solutions to the problems those challenges generate. Once you start using these tools, you'll wonder how you ever got along without them.

5. Each tool works.

Each Power Tool has undergone the "acid test." Real managers in real organizations have used it to solve real problems. These are not theoretical solutions or "it-all-depends" advice. The techniques you'll discover cut to the core of leadership and organizational distress. They have been tested in "pain clinics" around the country. They may need a bit of customizing to work for your patients, but they *will* work if you follow the instructions.

How Do I Use the Tools?

We have two answers to this question. First, you need to understand how they are structured to use them correctly. Second, you'll want to consult the Action Index on page 227 to select the right tool for your needs.

The Structure of the Tools

Each tool follows a consistent format, containing seven components presented in the same sequence.

1. Problems a Tool Solves. This is the "bottom line" of the tool. This section highlights the major benefits you'll realize in using the tool. These problems are taken directly from the Action Index and reflect the five management challenges described in Chapter 1. This section focuses on the *central* problems solved by the tool. Note that not all problem statements connected to a tool on the Action Index will necessarily appear in this section.

2. Implementation Parameters (in graphic form). Scan the icons at the left of the page for a quick overview before you use the tool. The graphic will be based on the chart shown below. For each issue, you will see the appropriate symbol.

Implementation Issues

- Support you'll need means the level of management that must either implement the tool or be in full support of it for the process to succeed. Some tools are "do-it-yourselfers" (example: *Balance*). Others require approval and support from top management (example: *Culture Print*).

Top management

Your manager

Do-it-yourself

- Implementation speed refers to the time it takes to get the tool fully up and operating.

Months

Weeks

Days/hours

- FULL EFFECT WILL BE FELT indicates the delay between implementation and full realization of the benefits.

In months

In weeks

In days/hours

- COMPLEXITY/CHALLENGE expresses the difficulty you might anticipate during implementation. Tools whose complexity/challenge is formidable should be applied with great thoughtfulness and care, and may require outside assistance in the form of a professional facilitator.

Formidable

Challenging

Easy

- APPROPRIATE TARGETS tells you who reaps the direct benefits. Often more than one level will be indicated.

Company

Division/team

Individual

- FINANCIAL INVESTMENT in the power tools is often very low and usually nonexistent. Even when "moderate" is indicated, your actual expenditures are highly discretionary.

Moderate

Little

None

- TIME OFF THE JOB suggests the amount of people-hours required for implementation. Some tools require little if any time away from the daily routine (example: *Brown Bag*). Others require a half day or more. Power Tools that involve entire teams (examples: *Aftermath, Vista*) often are in the "high" category.

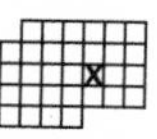

High

Medium

Low

3. Resources Needed. Some tools require a large meeting room, materials (flip charts, pens, etc.), or other resources. Whenever a tool requires the experience, insight, and skills of a professional facilitator, that is mentioned here.

4. Related Tools to Consult. Many Power Tools address multiple management problems, often in more than one of the five management challenge areas listed in Chapter 1. Several of the tools are also highly interdependent. Sometimes one helps you pull off another one. Sometimes they complement each other when implemented in tandem. Sometimes reading one can reveal insights into the successful application of another. For your convenience we cross-reference synergistic tools.

5. The Aim of the Tool. In this section you get a brief rationale of the tool's underlying logic. You learn why the tool solves the targeted problems.

6. How the Tool Works. This section reveals the nuts and bolts of the tool. This is the how-to, or blueprint, section. You may find questionnaires, agendas, possible discussion questions, sample scripts, or illustrative examples. The advice is presented in easy-to-follow steps. After reading this section you're ready to use the tool.

7. How Do I Make the Tool Work for Me? No two companies are exactly alike. No single problem presents itself identically to different managers. This section offers practical tips for adapting the tool to your company and its manifestation of the problems solved by the tool.

Now that you know how the tools work, turn to the Action Index and prepare to open your toolbox.

3 TOOLS FOR LEADERSHIP

Culture Print

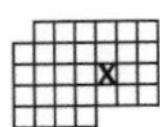

Resources needed:

None

Tools to consult:

Appraise for Success
Performance Pay
Great Expectations
Envision
Full-Circle Growth

What Problems Does Culture Print Solve?

- Employees don't feel enough emotional ownership for the goals or the strategy of this enterprise.
- The new people we hire are diluting the culture we've worked so hard to create.
- Employees complain that top management doesn't walk the talk.
- We're not all marching to the same beat. Sometimes it feels like we're not even all part of the same band.

What Is the Aim of This Tool?

With Culture Print you will define who you are as a company. You will create a positive statement of your culture. Your employees will help you identify the core values and beliefs that have brought you to where you are as an organization and will take you where you want to go.

The Culture Print defines your company so unmistakably that new employees will quickly discover what it takes to succeed and existing employees will have a reliable benchmark against which to measure their performance. It forms the foundation for a wide range of vital human-resource actions.

1. **Recruitment.** It gives you a clear profile of the kind of employee you want to look for when the time comes to add to your staff.
2. **Selection.** The Culture Print gives you a distinct statement of the criteria to use in

making your hiring decision. It tells you what skills to test, what to learn during interviews, and what questions to put to potential employees' references.

3. **Candidate self-screening.** Here's a way for you to make an unequivocal declaration to job candidates of the expectations they must fulfill once they accept an offer of employment. Consider the power of saying this at the end of an interview with a promising prospect: "Louisa would like to issue a job offer to you. But I don't want you to decide today on whether you will accept it. Take this Culture Print of our company home with you. Study it for one week. If after that time you conclude that you can thrive under the expectations in this document—and *only* if you can conclude that—call me to accept the offer."
4. **Orientation curriculum.** The Culture Print provides a focus for early training to help employees achieve the expectations in a particular core value area—such as customer service—and empowers them to get off to a good start.
5. **Training curriculum.** The Culture Print tells you what knowledge, skills, and attitudes your staff needs to improve on a regular basis to produce outstanding products and services.
6. **Performance review.** Culture Print tool enables you to devise a performance appraisal system that (1) is founded on your company's core values; (2) measures fulfillment of the performance expectations you have set within each of the core values; (3) is easily adapted for use in employee self-evaluation; (4) is easily understood and quickly accepted by both managers who will appraise with it and employees who will be appraised with it. (See *Appraise for Success.*)
7. **Employee development.** Going through the Culture Print steps is one way to generate the items for the 360-degree feedback instrument that is the basis for *Full-Circle Growth.*
8. **Mentoring and coaching.** The advice that your managers give to employees on career advancement and on performance improvement will be anchored in reality.
9. **Team building.** When you present the Culture Print to current employees, they will all be alerted at the same time to the same set of standards. It is likely to generate pride in their company and even greater support for a team effort than they have given in the past.

How Does Culture Print Work?

You will create a document that defines the work culture at your company. It identifies the core values that the company expects all employees to reflect in their performance. The Culture Print also specifies the performance expectations that fall within each core value, and thereby supports vital performance management systems.

Step 1: Get the support of top management.

This tool must be supported by the CEO on down through the management ranks. Don't attempt it without enthusiastic agreement among top managers that the Culture Print is needed and without a firm commitment to support the process outlined below.

Step 2: Convene a core values team.

Bring together a group of employees, supervisors, and middle-level managers to draft the core values of the company. Some might be volunteers, others nominated. The size and the makeup of this group will depend on the size of your company and on how widely representative you feel the team needs to be. Core values teams range between 4 and 30 employees. From the standpoint of performing the task with ease, 6 to 8 is an ideal number. If more people need to get involved, larger groups can be accommodated.

Step 3: Identify core values.

The chart on page 19 shows a sample of core values that teams have selected. A good number of core values to focus on is five to eight.

Your company may embrace every one of the values, but the aim here is to determine which are *core* values that deserve a prominent position in the eyes of employees. Don't mourn over the ones you leave out. You should be able to incorporate them into the performance expectations you'll create in Step 6.

Step 4: Gain approval of core values.

This is a key point of participation for the CEO and senior managers. They need to approve the chosen set of core values before the process can continue.

Sample Core Values

- Community service
- Continuous improvement
- Cost consciousness
- Customer focus
- Empowerment of employees
- Integrity
- Initiative/Innovation
- Leadership
- Positive work ethic
- Personal responsibility
- Productivity/Precision
- Professional development
- Quality
- Reliability
- Safety
- Teamwork
- Use of cutting-edge technologies
- Value to shareholders

Step 5: Define the core values.

Why is each core value important and what does it mean to your company? Write a paragraph explanining the significance of each core value so that there can be no question as to its rationale. This paragraph provides a foundation for the performance expectation teams will construct in Step 7. Here is a sample paragraph explaining the core value "productivity."

> Productivity is a central focal point for Interweld Industries. By continually increasing our productivity through hard work, dedication, and innovation, we are able to maintain our superior position in the marketplace. Productivity enables us to provide steady employment, enhance employee earning potential, and sustain growth.

Step 6: Convene one or more teams to create core performance expectations.

The core values team can serve this function. If the team is large enough, break it down into smaller performance expectation teams, one for every core value selected. A good number of participants in each performance expectation team is six to eight. If your core values team is too small to staff the number of performance expectation teams you need, you have two choices. One is to allow that team to develop the expectations for *all* core values. A better choice might be to recruit more employees for this step. This enables you to get more people involved and intensifies the focus given to each core value.

Step 7: Draft performance expectations.

Charge each performance expectation team with the task of listing the behaviors required of all employees in the core value(s) assigned to the team. (See *Great Expectations.*) If more than one performance expectation team works on this task, it will be necessary to coordinate their efforts to remove any undesirable duplication and to ensure that the results are consistent. It should be possible to emerge with a list that covers all employees regardless of job function. (Managers may need to be guided by an additional set of expectations that consider their supervisory and managerial duties.) As an example the team writing the expectations for the core value of "productivity" might emerge with the list below.

Step 8: Gain approval of performance expectations.

Again it is time for the CEO and top management, who should be connected to this process throughout, to approve progress—this time in the form of the list of performance expectations that cover the core values.

Productivity Expectations

1. **Strive to exceed established expectations for productivity.**
2. **Use time, equipment, and materials effectively and efficiently.**
   - Plan your job.
   - Stay focused on the task at hand; maintain a sense of urgency.
   - Run multiple operations when feasible.
   - Maximize unattended equipment operation.
   - Organize your workplace for maximum efficiency.
   - Do it right the first time; eliminate the need for reworking.
   - Make your communications clear, timely, and to the point.
   - Learn the most efficient and effective use of your equipment and materials.
3. **Engage in continuous improvement by suggesting and implementing improvements and cost savings in product design and function, work flow, efficiencies, customer service, communication, and other processes.**

Step 9: Publish your culture print.

The ultimate product of this process is a document that articulates the core values and the performance expectations related to those values. It is now time to publish that document. Before you actually take it to the printer, make two things happen. First, some individual or a small team needs to shape the work of the teams that have met to date into a coherent document. Second, present the document to all employees for their edification and for any input they want to provide. Following any changes made as a result of employee input, publish the Culture Print and distribute to the entire firm.

How Do I Make Culture Print Work for Me?

Designate focus teams to apply the Culture Print to the human resources functions you want to improve. You are now in a position to improve your recruitment, selection, orientation, training, mentoring, team building, and performance appraisals.

When you use Culture Print make sure you . . .

- Make maximum use of its power and its potential by applying it to every facet of your human resources system, from recruitment to exit interviews.
- Muster full and enthusiastic support of top management for this tool before proceeding.
- Involve as many employees as you can in the creation of the Culture Print. Everyone in the company should understand the final product and as many people as is humanly possible should accept it.
- Keep the Culture Print constantly visible in the organization. Review it annually for currency.

A partial sample of a Culture Print

One organization (referred to here as Interweld) followed the steps outlined above and emerged with a Culture Print based on seven core values. They chose productivity, quality, customer focus, personal responsibility, positive work ethic, teamwork, and safety. We showed how they developed "productivity" earlier. Their treatment of "customer focus" and "teamwork" appears on pages 22–23. Your core values teams and performance expectation teams will find this example helpful as a starting point.

Customer Focus as Core Value

Interweld Industries' reputation is built on product leadership. We offer our customers the highest-performing products in the precision manufacturing industry. Continued success and future growth depend on our ability to maintain close relationships with our customers and to offer total solutions to their problems. We pledge to provide our customers with exceptional care, ensuring that their needs are fully satisfied. We hold the following expectations of Interweld employees for customer satisfaction.

1. **Be customer-driven.**
   - Determine and meet the valid requirements of your customers.
   - Help them solve their problems, meet *their* customers' needs, grow their businesses, and remain profitable.
2. **Treat customers warmly, excitedly, appreciatively, professionally, and attentively, on the telephone and in person.**
   - Build personal bonds.
   - Stay in constant touch.
   - Seek to become an extension of their operation.
   - Remain sensitive to the cultural differences of our international customers.
3. **Remain constantly vigilant to eliminate sources of dissatisfaction for our customers.**
   - Don't mislead, manipulate, or deceive them.
   - Keep them informed.
   - Ask customers how we can improve.
   - Listen to their feedback, and act on it.
4. **Be sure customers needn't ask for something more than once before they get it.**
   - Don't let them lift a finger to get exceptional customer service.
   - Fill out the form, make the call, and otherwise go the extra mile.
   - Respond quickly to their needs.
5. **Continually strive to develop better, faster, and new ways to serve our customers.**
6. **When we fail to meet customer expectations, respond to problems quickly, happily, generously, remorsefully, and thankfully.**

Teamwork as Core Value

We believe in the positive impact of teamwork. We hire employees who are individually strong in their skills, education, and experiences. At the same time we recognize that only through the power of teamwork can we focus our individual contributions on organizational goals. Teamwork improves our efficiency and effectiveness. It allows us to serve our customers more responsively. It fosters harmony, allows individuals to develop to their fullest potential, and creates a more fulfilling workplace for our employees. It reflects a positive image to our customers, to our suppliers, and to our community. We hold the following expectations of Interweld employees for teamwork.

1. **Share information and knowledge with others.**
   - Impart needed information to coworkers and supervisors.
   - Share new ideas and recommend process improvements.
   - Express clearly your needs and expectations to related departments.
   - Keep supervisors informed of both your problems and your achievements.
   - Share lessons learned from failures and successes.
   - Advise your supervisor when you see opportunities for better use of the team.
2. **Support others.**
   - Obtain a thorough understanding of situations with other employees before you form an opinion.
   - Work through proper channels to bring about change.
   - Cooperate with the direction provided by your supervisor.
   - Strive to make "downstream" operations a success.
   - Provide exceptional internal customer service.
   - Be a positive role model to those around you.
   - Help and encourage employees in all departments and divisions.
3. **Respect others.**
   - Don't interrupt others or create distractions.
   - Treat others as equals; be considerate of them.
   - Don't gossip.
   - Don't be a chronic complainer.
   - Don't criticize others behind their backs.
   - Resolve disagreements directly and professionally.
   - Be on time for meetings.

Envision

Resources needed:

Flip charts
Markers
Post-it notes
Tape
Meeting room

Tools to consult:

Strategic Planner
Tactical Planner
Culture Print
Appraise for Success

What Problems Does Envision Solve?

- We're not all marching to the same beat. Sometimes it feels like we're not even all part of the same band.
- We lack direction and purpose.
- We need to put together a strategic plan.

What Is the Aim of This Tool?

Walt Disney said, "If you can dream it, you can do it." When he first saw the land on which he was going to build DisneyWorld, could he smell the popcorn popping, hear the laughter of the children, and see the fireworks exploding over Main Street? Disney passed away before the park was finished in 1972. At the opening day celebration, so the story goes, someone turned to Mrs. Disney and said, "I'm sorry that Walt was unable to see this." To which she replied, "Of course he saw this! How do you think it got here?"

Organizations today recognize the importance of having a vision statement, a document that communicates to employees, investors, customers, and the rest of the world what that organization aspires to become. The vision statement is intended to unify, to motivate, and to inspire confidence. A vision statement conveys two things to its reader: (1) the direction the organization is headed and (2) the guiding principles it will follow to get there. Some vision statements are no longer than one sentence; others take up many pages in an annual report. Vision statements provide the basis for strategic planning. (See *Strategic Plan* and *Tactical Plan.*)

A vision statement is distinguished from a mission statement in the following way. The mission statement describes what an organization does. The vision statement describes what it wants to do: its ambition and, perhaps, its guiding principles. For instance, a university may have the three-part mission of research, education, and community service. Its vision may be to be recognized as one of the top 50 research institutions in the nation.

Envision gives you the guidelines you need to assemble a vision statement appropriate for your enterprise—whether it is a project team or a multinational corporation. You can use it by yourself or include a large group of people.

How Does Envision Work?

The plan that follows is for the development of a two-part vision statement. Part 1 is the declaration of your aspiration. Part 2 is a revelation of the principles that will guide that aspiration and cause it to be reached.

Step 1: Assemble your vision team.

There is great value in involving a team of people to author the vision statement. The more hands take part in the creation, the better it will be and the more commitment you will muster for its realization.

Step 2: Write aspiration statements.

Give each person a pad of Post-it notes and have people write answers on them to as many of the following questions as they can. For ease in completing Step 3, ask them to include on each Post-it note the number of the question they are answering. A year from now . . .

1. What will our *market position* be?
2. What will *customers* say about us?
3. What will *competitors* say about us?
4. What will *employees* say about us?
5. What *standards* of excellence will we have achieved?
6. What *reputation* will we have in the marketplace?

Step 3: Post aspiration statements.

Place six large sheets of flip-chart paper on the walls corresponding to the six categories of aspiration statements. Have participants place their notes on the appropriate sheets.

Step 4: Write guiding principles.

Also on separate Post-it notes have participants write answers to as many of these questions as they want, again including the question number. As we strive to achieve the mission of this organization . . .

A. How will we deal with our *employees*?
B. How will we serve our *customers*?
C. How will we *conduct our business*?
D. What *organizational structure* will we use to relate to each other?
E. How will we treat our *environment*?
F. How will we relate to our *community*?

Encourage participants to think of such issues as decision making, teamwork, communication, authority, development, responsibility, and the short-term vs. the long-term planning as they propose their guiding principles.

Step 5: Post guiding principles.

Place six sheets of flip-chart paper on the walls corresponding to the six categories of guiding principles. Have participants place their notes on the appropriate sheets.

Step 6: Study the aspiration sheets and the guiding principles sheets.

Give participants 15 to 20 minutes to walk up to the 12 sheets of flip-chart paper and develop an overall impression of what they say about the corporate vision.

Step 7: Produce consensus aspirations and guiding principles.

Divide the group into six subgroups. Have each subgroup work on reducing one aspiration category to one consensus statement and three or four guiding principles. Allow the groups 20 to 30 minutes for each category assigned. When all group work is complete, have each one make a five-minute presentation on its choices. Then throw the floor open to questions and discussion.

Step 8: Draft your statement of aspiration.

This might be a single sentence or a paragraph. It should respond to all or a subset of the six questions posed in Step 3, but it does not have to refer directly to any one of them.

Step 9: Draft your statement of guiding principles.

You might write this as a single sentence or as a paragraph. It may be more effectively stated as a checklist of the various guiding principles in each of the six categories of Step 5.

Step 10: Use your vision statement.

The vision statement is more than a think piece. It becomes a living document that can be used profitably in these and other ways.

- Frame it for display throughout company offices, outlets, plants, and warehouses.
- Publish it in your annual report and in similar documents that reflect who you are.
- Publish it as a separate document for distribution.
- Introduce it at new employee orientation programs.
- Include items from it, as appropriate, on performance review forms. (See *Appraise for Success.*)
- Give employees the opportunity to give feedback to top management on whether the vision is genuinely held. Specifically, do members of top management reflect it in their behavior and are employees throughout the company rewarded for reflecting the vision in their behavior?
- Lead off all strategic planning initiatives with a review of the vision statement. (See *Tactical Plan* and *Strategic Plan.*)

How Do I Make Envision Work for Me?

Review the four excerpts of sample vision statements that companies have created for themselves on pages 28–29. Such statements can be a single sentence or multiple pages in a brochure. They are variously labeled "vision," "philosophy," and "values." Sometimes they are blended with the organization's mission—what it does. Notice how each of the examples takes a distinctive approach and emphasizes something different about the core values and beliefs of the organization.

"Premier Pharmaceuticals" Vision Statement

Our Vision

Our vision is to be a leader in the markets we serve and to be a major contributor to our worldwide parent company. We will achieve our vision through a diversified, highly motivated workforce; by satisfying and retaining loyalties of our external and internal customers; with an organization that is unencumbered by bureaucracy; by being environmentally responsible; and by being good corporate citizens in the communities in which we work and live.

"Excellent Electronics" Vision Statement

Our Philosophy

We strive for employee commitment by recognizing the potential for positive contributions from all employees, and by committing the organization to work toward the development of an atmosphere in which these contributions can, and will, be made. The following principles are intended as targets to be pursued at every facility.

- Focus on the positive behavior of employees.
- Encourage employee involvement in decisions.
- Communicate with employees in a timely and candid way, with emphasis on face-to-face communications.
- Compensate employees competitively, under systems that reward excellence.
- Provide training for organizational/individual success.
- Maintain effective performance-appraisal systems.
- Emphasize promotion from within throughout the company.
- Select managers and supervisors who demonstrate an appropriate blend of human relations skill and technical competence.

"Top Tools" Vision Statement

Our Vision

We strive to be both the manufacturer and the employer of choice in the precision tool and die industry.

"Unique Uniforms" Vision Statement

Our Philosophy

Our company philosophy is to serve our customers with a sense of competitive urgency. To be ethical in dealing with our customers and employees. To have the courage to face facts and to follow the facts even into unfamiliar and unexplored territory. To be consistent in quality and in performance. To pursue our business and our jobs with enthusiasm.

Our Vision

- To be recognized as a company that insists on absolute honesty and integrity in everything we do.
- To have a highly talented, diverse, and motivated team of partners who are compatible with our culture and enjoy what they do.
- To have a uniform rental presence in every city in the United States and Canada.
- To leverage our infrastructure to become a more valuable resource for our customers.
- To leverage our market presence to become the uniform people to other segments of the industry.
- To be the well-known leader and to have the highest market share in the geographic markets and all market segments we choose to serve.

Vista

Resources needed:

Meeting room with wall space
Magazine covers
Two flip charts
Pens and pads of paper
Two colors of Post-it notes

Tools to consult:

Strategic Planner

What Problems Does Vista Solve?

- Everyone in this company finds strategic planning frustrating. How can we improve it?
- Our managers have tunnel vision; how can I get them to focus on the strategic forces affecting our future?

What Is the Aim of This Tool?

Imagine putting a thousand-piece jigsaw puzzle together without seeing the picture of the completed puzzle on the box. The task would be very difficult. Yet that is precisely what many management teams try to do when they make crucial decisions and when they develop their strategic plans. They put a puzzle together without knowing what it is supposed to look like.

Most managers devote so much time to day-to-day operational issues that they lose sight of the big picture. They know every detail of what's going on in their operations and in operations throughout the company, but have only the vaguest sense of conditions developing outside the company that will determine the success of their decisions and their plans. And even if they do monitor outside forces, they still have their hands full just keeping up with today. Tomorrow is far off, unknown, and unpredictable.

Vista helps you and your team conduct the most vexing part of strategic planning: trend analysis. With this tool you will examine and anticipate the most likely threats and opportunities affecting your industry generally and your company specifically. This trend analysis can then be used as the basis for a more meaningful strategic plan. Even if you're not doing a strategic plan this tool will enable you and other managers to make your daily actions and decisions more in tune with the realities of the market.

How Does Vista Work?

Vista is used early on in the strategic planning sequence when it becomes necessary to analyze the major trends affecting your company. (See *Strategic Planner.*) Vista is based on the premise that the major cover stories of trade and popular magazines published over the preceding 12-month period yield a clear and fairly complete picture of the major trends affecting any company. This technique is called content analysis and is used in various forms by many trend watchers.

Since Vista is primarily a strategic planning tool, top-level managers are the most appropriate participants. However, when Vista is used primarily to help employees see the big picture, the tool can be used with any group and any type of team, department, or company.

In the following steps, the actual group exercises are in Steps 4 and 5. They take a total of about two hours. But the preparation will make those two hours most beneficial.

Step 1: Select the news sources most appropriate for your trend analysis.

Four categories of trends to focus on are (1) those going on in society at large, (2) those affecting your specific industry, (3) those impacting the markets you serve, and (4) those happening in business in general. For the first category, sources include magazines published for a general audience that feature stories affecting large segments of society: *Time, Newsweek,* and *U.S. News and World Report.* Industry sources include the major magazines, newsletters, or journals published by your trade association. Business sources would be the periodicals published for the general business audience, such as *Fortune, Forbes, Business Week,* and *American Demographics.* You might even add the covers from a few best-selling self-help and business books.

Step 2: Photocopy a sampling of the front covers or front pages of these news sources.

Assign this step to two or three managers. At the local library, have them make copies of the covers of the preceding 12 months of issues of the monthly periodicals selected for your trend analysis. If you have selected more than one weekly magazine, the managers should pick and choose from the issues to avoid information overload. This procedure should yield somewhere between 100 to 150 covers. The managers will bring the completed collection to the meeting where the remaining steps are to be completed.

Step 3: Prepare the room for the Vista session.

Place tables and chairs in a horseshoe arrangement with two flip charts at the open end of the horseshoe. At the top of one of the flip-chart sheets write the word "Threats." Write the word "Opportunities" atop the other sheet. Tape copies of the cover stories to the back and side walls of the room. Organize the covers in three sections: society, industry, business. Place the covers randomly within each section. Don't worry about chronology or topic. Leave enough space between the tables and the walls so that participants can stand or stroll along the walls without bumping into tables or chairs. Place a pen, two pads of Post-it notes of different colors, and a pad of paper on the table at each participant's place.

Step 4: Conduct the session.

Set aside three hours of uninterrupted time for the session. On the opposite page we recommend some opening remarks for presenting this exercise during a strategic planning session.

Step 5: Subgroups summarize the findings.

Break the group into two smaller groups—one studying threats, the other opportunities. Each group studies the Post-it notes on its sheet. The groups are given one hour to summarize their sheets. A spokesperson from each group then makes a 10-minute presentation on the major threats or opportunities affecting the company.

How Do I Make Vista Work for Me?

Stick to the agenda of trend analysis, not action planning.

The limited agenda of Vista is trend analysis—developing a big picture of threats and opportunities. Leave discussions of what we

Sample Opening Remarks for Vista Session

At this step in creating our strategic plan, we turn our attention to the most dominant trends affecting us. What are the threats and opportunities out there? How is the world changing, and what can we do to take advantage of it? For the next three hours we're going to discuss these questions and conduct a trend analysis.

But we're not going to sit around and speculate or guess. We're going to analyze data reflecting societal and business trends—the information you see on the side and back walls.

Take 30 minutes to walk around the room. Look at all the covers. Look for underlying trends. Seek relationships between and among them. Jot down notes and impressions as they occur to you. Please don't talk while you're studying the covers. We don't want your impressions to be affected by anyone else's.

When you're finished, jot down the major threats and opportunities you see for us. Use the blue Post-it notes for threats; the yellow for opportunities. Place your notes on the two large sheets labeled "Threats" and "Opportunities" at the front of the room.

should *do* about trends to the tool *Strategic Planner*. Resist the temptation of the group to jump to responsive actions without using a planning tool.

Videotape the discussion sessions.

All employees should understand the trends affecting the company. Unfortunately, not all employees can attend the Vista session. Absent employees can benefit from the session by watching the video. Have the videographer begin the tape with a slow close-up pan of the magazine covers and end with the group summary presentations. At most, the whole tape will be thirty minutes long.

Consider other sources of trend data.

In addition to covers of periodicals, you might include a bit of textual information such as annual reports or strategic plans from major customers. More information might come in the form of briefings—either live or in print—from customers, suppliers, accountants, attorneys, or bankers.

Develop a "trend watch" within your company.

Establish a physical or electronic bulletin board where any employee can post "blips" (short stories, anecdotes, or news summaries) that they believe represent trends worth tracking. Use the collected information at your next Vista session. Discussions in *Brown Bag* seminars are another source for a trend watch.

Strategic Planner

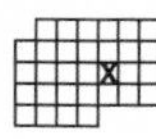

Resources needed:

Facilitator
Flip charts
¾-inch colored sticky dots
Meeting room

Tools to consult:

Envision
Vista
Tactical Planner

What Problems Does Strategic Planner Solve?

- I'm taking over a new organization that needs help. Where do I start in order to turn things around?
- We're not all marching to the same beat. Sometimes it feels like we're not even all part of the same band.
- We need to figure out better ways of doing things around here.

What Is the Aim of This Tool?

Truly successful organizations have four things in common. First, the people within those organizations are unified by a common *vision*, or view of the future. Second, they have devised a commonly understood and widely accepted *strategy* for achieving the vision. Third, they agree on the employee *performance requirements* that are needed to execute the strategy. Fourth, they set in motion a *plan* to see that the performance requirements are fulfilled.

Strategic Planner is a tool that can be used to make sure your organization achieves these four conditions. It empowers your staff to act upon the vision it shares for the future. It provides the blueprint you need both to seize opportunities presented to your organization and to surmount whatever challenges may stand in the way. It yields a strategy with five essential qualities:

1. The strategy is initiated by leadership.
2. The strategy is shared and supported throughout the organization.

3. The strategy is comprehensive and detailed.
4. The strategy is positive and inspiring.
5. The strategy is monitored for success.

How Does Strategic Planner Work?

Strategic Planner often takes the form of a retreat conducted off-site for the senior management of a company. You are encouraged, however, to involve as many layers of management and employees as you feel will positively contribute to your organization's plan. The retreat requires one to two days, depending on how task-oriented the group remains and how much of the work of the plan is accomplished in advance of the retreat. The retreat should be led by an outsider, preferably a skilled facilitator. The meeting room should be bright and airy with plenty of wall space for posting large sheets of flip-chart paper.

Take the planning group through the following steps and record the results of each one on large sheets of flip-chart paper.

Step 1: Establish your corporate mission.

A mission statement is typically one sentence to one paragraph in length. It answers most or all of these questions: What business are we in? What do we do or achieve? For whom? Where? When?

Step 2: Establish your corporate vision.

A vision statement can be anywhere from one sentence to several pages in length. It answers most or all of these questions: Where are we headed? What are our aspirations? What do we intend to become? What future do we desire? What core values and essential beliefs will guide us? (See *Envision* for the actual process of creating a vision statement.)

Step 3: Conduct an external environment assessment.

What are the major trends affecting our business? These trends are occurring in three areas: the society at large, our industry and the markets we serve, and overall business. (See *Vista* for our recommended way to perform a trend analysis.) Which of these trends are threats? Which are opportunities?

Step 4: Conduct an internal assessment.

What is unique about us? What do we do extremely well? What do we do poorly? What are our distinctive competencies? What are our distinctive weaknesses? In sum, what are our advantages and disadvantages in this market?

Step 5: Set goals.

How should we respond to the analysis to this point? Namely, what should we be doing that we're not doing now to . . .

- Achieve our mission
- Reach our vision
- Respond to external opportunities
- Counteract external threats
- Build on internal advantages
- Shore up internal disadvantages

The answers to these questions are the goals of your strategic plan.

Step 6: Prioritize goals.

Which of the goals should get first attention? The value in prioritizing goals is that the actions taken to achieve the higher-priority goals often contribute substantially to the achievement of lower-priority goals.

Step 7: Perform a force-field analysis on each goal.

What forces act against accomplishment of the goal and are considered *constraining* forces? What forces act in favor of the goal and are considered *supportive* forces? List all such forces on a sheet of flip-chart paper.

Step 8: Develop action plans for achieving each goal.

For each goal, *what* actions will minimize the negative forces and maximize the positive forces uncovered in the force-field analysis? *Who* will have the responsibility for each action? *When* will it be begun, or when will it be accomplished? What *resources* will required to pull it off? Who must understand and *support* the action?

Step 9: Implement the actions.

Once you return to the office, have the prioritized listing of the goals from Step 6 typed up and given to planning team members.

Each action plan should appear separately and go to the team members assigned to that plan.

Step 10: Commit to a process of accountability for the action plans.

Type up the entire collection of individual actions from the several action plans, arranged in the chronological order of their intended accomplishment. This format allows for easy monitoring of progress of the total planning effort. The strategic planning team and the task groups that may subsequently be formed to accomplish particular goals should meet on a regular basis to review developments.

How Do I Make Strategic Planner Work for Me?

Here are some tips to improve the quality of outcomes you get from this tool.

Review the mission statement first.

If you need to create one from scratch, try this method. Have everyone in the group write a proposed one-sentence mission statement on a Post-it note. Number them and place them on the wall where everyone can see them. Let people vote for the statement(s) they believe best captures the essence of the organization. Refine the winner(s) into a consensus statement everyone can accept.

Even if you have a vision statement, review it.

Spend some time discussing how well the group believes it is reflected in everyday operations. In other words, ask the question "Do we walk our talk?" Use *Envision* to improve on the existing vision statement or to create a new one if you see that need. Make certain that any changes in the vision statement are communicated to employees.

Consider the external environment before the planning session.

An external environment assessment is a time-consuming exercise (see *Vista*), and you can involve a larger number of people in performing it than you may wish to invite to the retreat.

Create and prioritize goals in separate steps.

Have people brainstorm goals without judging their value. Next, look for possibilities to combine similar goals under single headings. Once you're satisfied that you have a list of distinctively different goals written on a sheet of flip-chart paper at the front of the room, issue to participants a number of sticky dots equal to about one third of the total number of goals. Have them come forward to place their dots next to the goals they believe are most vital for the success of the organization.

Record action plans in a standard format.

Use a format like this to record action plans on large sheets of flip-chart paper at the front of the room.

Action Plan

What Action to Take	Who	When	Resources	Support Needed

Follow through.

The groups that are most successful in achieving their action plans are those that (1) have broad and active participation in the strategic plan, as opposed to groups that are overly influenced or even bullied by the leader throughout the planning retreat; (2) perform the most thorough force-field analyses in Step 7; (3) are careful not to be overly ambitious in the extent of their action plans or overly optimistic as to when the plans can be completed; (4) give as many people as possible a piece of the action in carrying out the action plans, including many people who were not at the retreat; (5) communicate the shape of the action plans, any revisions to the visions, and all other tangible outcomes from the planning session as soon as possible to those who did not attend the retreat; (6) monitor very closely the achievement of the plan (Step 10).

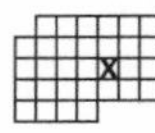

Resources needed:

Flip-chart pad
At least one flip-chart easel
Markers
Pad of 3x5-inch Post-it notes for each person
Masking tape
¾-inch colored sticky dots
Meeting room

Tools to consult:

Envision
Strategic Planner

Tactical Planner

What Problems Does Tactical Planner Solve?

- We need to figure out a better way of doing things around here.
- We need to get new initiatives under way quickly.
- I'm taking over an organization that needs help; where do I start in order to turn things around?

What Is the Aim of This Tool?

Human organizations, from teams to entire companies, are subject to entropy. That's a fancy way of saying that they're always heading toward decay and disorganization. If they don't work hard at staying fixed, they'll fall apart. If they don't refresh themselves, they'll tire out. And if they don't innovate, they'll stagnate.

One of your more challenging tasks as a manager is to figure out what it will take to keep your team or company alive and intact—marching down the same road to the same tune, with minimal conflict and with maximum excitement. Tactical Planner is one of the tools in this book that can make your group more productive and more creative.

This tool works best in teams or in companies that are already well established but need a shot in the arm or a bit of fine-tuning. Unlike some of the more elaborate strategic planning models, it can be completed in as little as a day. (See *Strategic Planner* for a more comprehensive planning tool, one that takes more time and is more appropriate a new organization or one that is preparing to move in a totally new direction.)

How Does Tactical Planner Work?

In today's volatile business world, organizations need to be constantly open to a redefinition of their purposes, a redirection of their priorities, and a rejuvenation of their energy. Tactical Planner enables you to accomplish this for your team or your company through a series of well-defined steps. These steps should be performed in a retreat setting away from screaming calendars and ringing telephones.

Step 1: Identify the group that will help you create the Tactical Planner.

One of the strengths of this tool is that you can involve many people in creating the blueprint you will be asking them to support. It can easily accommodate up to 50 or 60 people, if you value such broad participation.

Step 2: Identify focus areas for tactical planning.

This tool empowers you to revitalize the results being achieved in key organizational focus areas such as the ones listed below. You may want to use some of these, but don't be limited by this list. Try to select no more than a total of six focus areas. The average number selected—and a good number to work with—is four or five

- Change
- Collections
- Community relations
- Cost control
- Customer service
- Employee development
- Engineering
- Growth
- Human resources
- Marketing
- Organization
- Orientation
- Pricing
- Production
- Profitability
- Programs
- Recruitment
- Retention
- Safety/security
- Selling

- Space
- Strategy
- Teamwork
- Technology
- Training

Step 3: Select a retreat location.

You'll need a large meeting room with plenty of wall space for posting large sheets of flip-chart paper. Any food served to the group should be buffet style to avoid losing time to slowly served meals.

Step 4: Review the group's vision statement.

See *Envision* for a tool you can use to revise your current vision statement, if appropriate, or create one from scratch at the meeting. To save time, come with copies of a current vision statement for each participant. By opening the retreat with this review, you point everyone in the same direction.

Step 5: Generate "from-to" statements in each focus area.

After explaining what each selected focus area means, give participants 15 minutes to consider what changes need to occur in each of them: *from* what *to* what. Have them write on separate Post-it notes at least one from-to statement in each area to express how they believe the organization needs to move. Consider the examples in the chart below.

Place large sheets of flip-chart paper on the wall, and write the title of one focus area on each. Have participants stick their from-to statements on the appropriate sheets.

Sample From-To Statements

Focus Area	From-To Statement
People	*From* an organization where talented people leave *to* one where the best and brightest stay.
Marketing	*From* an office that markets by department *to* one that markets actively across service lines and departments.
Strategy	*From* strategy as a concern only for top management *to* jointly written goals that are understood and supported by all.

Step 6: Form from-to task groups; get reports.

Once everyone has written their from-to statements, call a break during which all can mill around in front of the flip-chart sheets to get a sense of what they say. At some point ask participants to move to the area in front of the sheet that most interests them. There they will form a task group. (Encourage those not immediately attracted to an area to wait and help to keep the focus groups somewhat equal in size. Also attempt to distribute people from various departments throughout the task groups.)

Give the task groups about 45 minutes to perform the following task: "Pore through all the from-tos on the sheet. Combine and cluster them so that you emerge with consensus from-to statements that best represent what participants want to achieve in that area. There should be as few as possible, no more than a half dozen."

When task groups are finished, have them make a five-minute presentation to the larger assembly on their choices for consensus from-tos. Everyone in the assembly should feel free to comment. Sometimes task group results are heavily biased and do not represent a fair consensus of the assembly. Do not proceed any further without eliminating as much of that bias as possible.

Step 7: Prioritize the focus areas.

Ask participants to rank the areas. Total the number of first-, second-, and third-place votes each focus area receives. Identify the top-priority focus area.

Step 8: Perform force-field analyses on from-to statements in the top-priority focus area; get reports.

Write the consensus from-to statements on separate flip-chart sheets. Once again, ask participants to distribute themselves, evenly if possible, among the statements. Ask the groups to perform a force-field analysis on the statement they chose.

On the left side of the force field, the group identifies the forces that support its achievement. On the other side of the force field, the group identifies the restraining forces that are acting to prevent the from-to from being achieved. The groups will need 30 to 45 minutes to discuss the from-to and to complete the analysis. Have groups work on large sheets of flip-chart paper. A sample force-field analysis for one of the from-to statements quoted earlier is shown on the next page.

From an Organization That Loses Talent *to* One Where the Best and Brightest Stay

Supportive Forces ⇒	⇐ Restraining Forces
■ Possibility of diverse experiences ■ Some recognition of talents and victories ■ Our response to lifestyle preferences; flex-work schedules ■ Renewed emphasis on technology ■ We try to listen ■ Professional environment ■ Stimulating environment ■ Growth potential ■ Candor about our problems and genuine desire to solve them ■ Good mentoring and counseling	■ Attractive outside options ■ Clients woo our best ■ Poorly communicated benefits of staying ■ Poor work-scheduling process ■ Hasn't historically been a fun place to work ■ Tradition of two-or-three-years-and-out has taken hold ■ Administrative staff not treated as professionals ■ Our clients are tough to work with; highly demanding ■ Shortage of positive role models among senior managers ■ Too few opportunities for promotion ■ High-pressure environment ■ "Sweat shop" legacy ■ Senior managers work like dogs ■ Break in the trust ■ Culture of more "whiner" language than "winner" language ■ Poor prospects for work-life balance apparent to younger staff ■ Our selection process may be bringing in those destined to leave ■ Training and development opportunities are severely limited

Give each group ten minutes to present its findings and to allow the entire assembly to critique its work.

Step 9: In the same way, perform force-field analyses on the from-to statements for the second-highest-priority focus area; get reports.

You may choose to continue with force-field analyses until all statements have been analyzed. Alternatively you may choose to skip this step and begin action planning on the top-priority focus area. This decision will be made in the context of the time remaining in your schedule and the number of focus areas you have chosen. If you run out of time before all force fields are complete, you can return to the lower-priority areas at a subsequent retreat or back in the office in smaller focus groups.

Step 10: Create action plans.

You may wonder why we didn't direct you to this step as soon as the from-to statements were identified. The reason is to avoid the mistake that so many planners make of moving directly from a goal to the actions they plan to take to achieve that goal. What is the error in this? They have no way of knowing, other than through intuition, that the actions they propose will indeed achieve the goal. Doing a force-field analysis provides the necessary intermediate step—the step of identifying *what is keeping the goal from being achieved.*

What actions will lead to attainment of a goal? The actions that overcome the obstacles currently standing in the way of goal achievement ("restraining forces"), and perhaps actions that take advantage of existing opportunities to build on current strengths ("supportive forces"). So that's what you're looking for in this step: actions that will counteract the restraining forces and build on the supportive ones.

If you have lots of time, have the whole group do the action plan for each focus area. Each action plan will take 30 to 45 minutes to complete. If you need to move the agenda along more quickly, have smaller groups work on action plans for separate focus areas concurrently.

Have groups work on large sheets of flip-chart paper. The table on page 46 shows one format you can use to record the action plans. The example is a partial action plan for the focus area

Action Plan for Retaining Talented Employees

What Action to Take	Who	When
1. Design a presentation to all staff on the benefits of employment here in comparison to outside options.	______	1/17
2. Hire a person full time to handle scheduling and other actions that will ease some of the pressure.	______	1/29
3. Initiate leadership skills and interpersonal skills training for senior management.	______	2/12
4. Conduct a seminar on stress-management techniques.	______	2/28
5. Invite administrative staff to next management retreat.	______	4/17
6. Initiate a career-mapping program.	______	3/15

"People," concentrating on retaining talented employees. The plan could be published separately as an action plan for retaining employees, or it could be incorporated into the other action plans generated from force-field analyses of other from-to statements in the "People" focus area.

Step 11: Assign action plan responsibilities.

Once you draft all action plans, ask people to commit themselves to work on one or more of the plans. One way to do this is to post the plans on the walls and have participants walk around the room. Give participants one or more light-colored sticky dots on which they can write their initials, and ask them to place them in the "Who" column next to at least one action (as shown above). Finally, have participants meet in front of the action plan in which they will be most active to elect a leader and to schedule a first organizational meeting back in the office.

Step 12: Commit to follow up.

Before you leave the retreat, lead a discussion of what participants will do to ensure that the action plans are achieved. You might begin the accountability process by having the head of the organization appear at each initial action plan meeting to pledge his or her support. Another way to ensure answerability is to hold a monthly meeting of action plan leaders where each one reports to the organizational leader on what is getting done. Also, be sure to schedule a half-day follow-up session about three months down the road where the entire planning group can learn about and comment on progress.

How Do I Make Tactical Planner Work for Me?

Keep these tips in mind to get the most out of this tool:

1. Appoint a facilitator to lead the retreat. Perhaps this person should be a professional process consultant. Certainly the facilitator should not be a member of the group going through the retreat because of the possibility for exerting undue influence.
2. Involve as many people as possible for the sake of buy-in. Bear in mind, though, that if you choose only a few focus areas with a large group, task groups assigned to emerge with consensus from-to statements for the two focus areas may be unwieldy.
3. Take Step 11 seriously. Without appropriate pressure, action plans often take a backseat to the daily grind.
4. Choose too few rather than too many focus areas to work on.
5. If you limited yourself to two focus areas, you can easily complete the entire process in one day. If you choose more focus areas, you can either add time to the retreat or plan to complete part of the process back in the office. You can reduce an excessive number of focus areas by combining areas that are similar. You can also shorten time by aiming for only one or two from-to statements per focus area.
6. Don't allow overly ambitious action plans to be created. It's demoralizing for a group to miss deadlines that should have been placed further in the future.

Typical agenda for two focus areas

The agenda on the next page will work for a highly focused, task-oriented group. On a second day you can complete another three focus areas. By taking advantage of some of the shortcuts suggested above, up to seven focus areas can be completed in two days.

Typical Agenda

8:00–8:30 A.M.	Review the group's vision statement. (Step 4)
8:30–8:45 A.M.	Generate from-to statements in each focus area. (Step 5)
8:45–9:45 A.M.	Form from-to task groups; get reports. (Step 6)
9:45–10:00 A.M.	Break.
10:00–10:15 A.M.	Prioritize the focus areas. (Step 7)
10:15–11:45 A.M.	Perform force-field analyses on from-to statements in the top-priority focus area; get reports. (Step 8)
11:45 A.M.–12:45 P.M.—	Lunch.
12:45–2:15 P.M.	Perform force-field analyses on the from-to statements for the second-highest-priority focus area; get reports. (Step 9)
2:15–2:30 P.M.	Break.
2:30–4:00 P.M.	Create action plans. (Step 10)
4:00–4:30 P.M.	Assign plan responsibilities. (Step 11)
4:30–4:45 P.M.	Commit to follow up. (Step 12)

Great Expectations

Resources needed:

None

Tools to consult:

Culture Print
Appraise for Success
Lemons and Oranges
Team Builder
Performance Fixer

What Problems Does Great Expectations Solve?

- Not enough people are following my lead.
- More people around here need to know exactly what I expect of them.
- I have a problem performer on my hands.

What Is the Aim of This Tool?

We often ask employees of the companies with which we work, "How many of you believe you know one hundred percent of your boss's expectations for your performance?" If there are 100 employees in the room, there's a good chance that not even one hand will go up. When we ask, "How many of you believe you know ninety-five percent of your boss's expectations?" we may see half a dozen hands. When the percentage falls to 75 percent, as many as two-thirds of the hands in the room will be raised. But even at 50 percent not all of the audience has typically been stirred.

Can you say with certainty that your employees would report better knowledge of your expectations of them? Even though they may all have job descriptions of *what* they do, do they know *how*, *why*, *when*, *where*, and *to what degree of quality* the job is to be done? For instance, a waiter has been trained in taking food orders from customers, serving that food, and collecting the bill. Does that waiter also know not to call customers "you guys," not to serve water glasses by holding them at the top, and not to give the check automatically to the man when a man and woman are dining together?

Any of five factors may be preventing you from being explicit with your performance requirements. Check off the one below that is the best explanation for your employees not understanding clearly your expectations of them.

___I'm not the "great communicator." Too often I keep things to myself that others should know about.
___I don't have the time to be explicit about my performance standards.
___I don't know myself what I expect of employees, either because I'm not getting clear signals from upper management or because I've never given this idea much thought.
___I assume that people—especially experienced people—should know my requirements of them.
___I'm concerned about the consequences of being up-front with my performance expectations. I may not want to put more pressure on my employees. I might dread what they would tell me to do with my expectations. I may like the current confusion. I may be afraid I'll have to reward them when they achieve a known goal.

Great Expectations helps you overcome the barriers that have kept you from being clear with your employees. It shines a brighter light on your relations with them. It tells them exactly what they need to do to succeed on the job. It rules out the possibility of ignorance as the cause of employee, and team, failure.

How Does Great Expectations Work?

Follow this recipe to write performance expectations for an employee or for a group of employees who function as a team or perform similar duties.

Step 1: Plan to cover all vital performance categories.

Consider these performance areas when you write your expectations.

- How employees communicate with and report to you
- How employees relate to your boss
- How employees relate to colleagues and other departments
- How employees supervise subordinates
- How employees serve customers
- Quality and quantity of employees' work
- Employees' work and personal habits, such as dress, grooming, or cleanliness

The average number of expectations distributed throughtout these categories typically is between 25 and 35.

Step 2: Begin expectation statements with verbs.

State your requirements so that they start with words such as *create, carry out, be, treat, remain, allow, strive, respond, use, engage in, work, grow, possess, behave, adhere to, fulfill, ensure, extend, assume, safeguard, share, support, respect, operate, follow, perform, report, arrive, deliver, pitch in, suggest, avoid, learn, fix,* and *help.*

Step 3: Make each expectation so specific that there is no room for doubt or incorrect interpretation.

In some cases you need to give examples of what you want. For example, the expectation "Behave in a professional manner" will be of little value unless you cite types of behavior that you deem professional.

Step 4: Get outside help to articulate your expectations.

Consult these sources: the job description, past performance appraisals, your boss, your colleagues, your customers, as well as your impressions about how well each employee's job is being done.

Step 5: Get outside help to evaluate your expectations.

Go over your list with your boss, your colleagues, and possibly your human resources office before presenting it to employees. Be certain your expectations are clear, realistic, consistent, fair, and legal as well as appropriate to the job and necessary for quality

Performance Expectation Examples

Poor Example	Why It's a Poor Example	Good Example
"Behave in a professional manner."	Subject to different interpretations	"Behave in professional manner by . . . [give examples]."
"Be honest with me."	Too general	"Tell me whenever you disagree with one of my actions."
"Dependability."	Not a sentence	"Do your work on time and to specifications."
"Be available to work on weekends without advance notice."	Could be illegal if it violates employee's right to practice his or her religion	None
"Contribute time to community service organizatons."	Depending on the job responsibility, may not be necessary for quality output	None

output. In the chart above are examples of bad and good performance expectation statements. (See *Culture Print* for other examples.)

How Do I Make Great Expectations Work for Me?

- Use expectations to communicate with the employees who are directly responsible to you. Be careful how you present them. Give this rationale: You want to be fairer with them than you have been in the past when your expectations were not as openly stated. Explain the expectations thoroughly, giving examples of each one. Listen to their concerns or questions with patience and understanding. Expect them to be suspicious, anxious, and defensive. They may also be overwhelmed by what they see as new requirements from you. Emphasize that the only thing new is your honesty—don't choke on the word. You've always had these expectations. You just haven't been so forthcoming with them. (See *Culture Print* if you want to communicate expectations throughout an entire company.)

- This is a good time to ask your employees to communicate their expectations of you. That is, what do they need from you in order to fulfill your expectations of them? Give them some time to think about this question—at least the same amount of time you took to shape your list.
- Use your expectations of employees as the basis for performance reviews. (See *Appraise for Success.*) You should also use the expectations they create of you to get regular feedback from them on the effectiveness of your supervision. (See *Lemons and Oranges.*)
- Use expectations to hire. Perhaps the greatest cause of failure in new hires, and when new teams are formed among current employees, is that people begin assignments without a complete understanding of what is expected of them. When you interview job prospects make your expectations known in order to help prospects decide whether the position is one in which they can thrive. See how to use expectations to get teams off to the right start in *Team Builder.*
- You will increase the ownership employees feel of the expectations if you allow them to create the first draft of the performance expectations. You will likely be amazed at how little you need to add to their list in order to refine it and emerge with a final set of performance expectations.

Resources needed:

None

Tools to consult:

Gripe Session
Sell It

Lead with Your Ears

What Problems Does Lead with Your Ears Solve?

- I'm taking over an organization that needs help; where do I start in order to turn things around?
- Employees don't feel enough ownership of the goals or strategy of this enterprise.
- We need to figure out better ways of doing things around here.
- Employees aren't sending good news, bad news, or great ideas up the line.

What Is the Aim of This Tool?

This tool is based on the advice of the former secretary of state Dean Rusk: "The best way to persuade someone is with your ears—by listening to them." In other words, listening is a vital leadership action that gains respect, knowledge, and influence for you.

Lead with Your Ears is especially valuable when you move into a new leadership situation. It enables you to learn as much as possible about the people you are to lead—their expectations, their needs, their hopes, their values, and their fears. This approach encourages and empowers them to help you succeed. It also gives them an outlet for their ideas and concerns that they may not have had before. Finally, you earn enormous esteem in a new assignment when you do *not* walk in the door announcing "There are going to be some changes around here" before learning what those changes should be.

It is important for leaders to be good listeners throughout their tenure, but it is most important to "lead with your ears" when you first meet your new staff.

How Does Lead with Your Ears Work?

Whenever you take over the reins of a team, committee, office, department, division, plant, or company, begin this process before you set any weighty goals, make any strategic decisions, or take any decisive actions.

Step 1: Announce your plans to carry through this process.

Describe the following steps to the entire group. Give them an opportunity to comment on it and to suggest ideas for successful implementation.

Step 2: Select individuals to interview.

If your leadership responsibility is limited to a team, committee, or office, you may be able to interview everyone; if you head up a department, division, plant, or company, you may interview key staff members and perhaps a random selection of others. In large groups you might even accept volunteer interviewees.

Step 3: Conduct interviews.

A length of 30 to 45 minutes is sufficient. Ask interviewees lots of questions about themselves, their work, and their perceptions of the group. Show your interest in their opinions by listening to the answers and taking notes.

On page 56 is a sample list of questions to use in your interviews. There are too many questions on the list for a 30- to 45-minute interview, and not all of these questions are relevant to every leadership situation, so pick and choose carefully according to your needs. (See *One-Finger Questions* for additional ideas.)

Take advantage of the interview by following up most responses with further questions that probe more deeply and yield an even richer harvest than the original question.

Step 4: Analyze interview results.

Write down what you hear. Go back to interviewees who can help fill any holes or clear up any confusion in your data. Select additional interviewees who might be able to do the same.

Sample Interview Questions

1. "Describe your job to me."
2. "What are the most difficult parts of your job?"
3. "What do you like most about your job?"
4. "What do you like least about your job?"
5. "What are the greatest challenges you face in creating quality outcomes?"
6. "In the past year what is the greatest success you had in your job?"
7. "In the past year what is the greatest failure you had in doing your job?"
8. "If there is one training program we could send you to help you do your job better, what would it be?"
9. "With whom do you work most closely in doing your job?"
10. "With whom do you collaborate best?"
11. "With whom around here you do have a relationship in need of growth? How do you suggest that growth be attained?"
12. "What ideas do you have for doing things better, faster, or cheaper around here?"
13. "What do you need from the person in my position in order for you to do your job effectively?"
14. "What is one thing the last person in my position could have done to help you be a greater success?"
15. "In what particular ways do you add value to this team [committee, etc.]? What would we lose immediately if you were replaced tomorrow?"
16. "Do you think this team [committee, etc.] is headed in the right direction? If not, what new direction do you suggest?"
17. "What ideas do you have for improving communication on this team [committee, etc.]?"
18. "How could we make better use of your interests, talents, and skills?"
19. "How could we make better use of the interests, talents, and skills of any of your colleagues?"
20. "What questions do you have for me?"

Step 5: Announce results.

Assemble the people you interviewed. (In the case of large organizations, you may want to go beyond the circle of interviewees for this meeting or series of meetings.) Tell them what you heard and what you learned. Ask whether they feel that your conclusions accurately represent the "state of the union." Solicit their help in correcting any misperceptions. Finally, tell them what goals, decisions, and actions the data appear to indicate.

You may be ready to announce specific initiatives, or you may need to go back to the drawing board for a few days or a few weeks before mapping a new direction. That new direction might take one of several forms: strategic planning sessions, reorganization, restructuring, reengineering, training programs, team-building retreats, and other action plans. Other tools that might be helpful at this point include *Envision, Tactical Planner, Strategic Planner,* and *Team Builder.*

Step 6: Assign tasks.

The final step in the process is to meet selectively with interviewees and others to get their opinions of your plans, and to enlist the cooperation of each participant regarding his or her specific role in fulfilling those plans. You also want their candid opinions of the likely success of the plans.

How Do I Make Lead with Your Ears Work for Me?

- It is sometimes difficult to keep people talking. When people wind down and you want to hear more, simply repeat or paraphrase the final words of their last sentence. To an employee mentioning an encounter with an abusive customer your response might be, "The customer really got to you." Expect the employee to wind up again with, "You bet! And . . . "
- When the speaker is talking about an especially emotional experience, statements of empathy work well to help him or her continue to ventilate. Try this: "That must be [exciting/challenging/painful/difficult/awful] for you!"
- Certain questions can help to keep you on the listening end of your interviews with employees. Try these: "Really?" "And?" "What else?" "Who else?" "How did you feel about that?" "What can I do to help?"
- Commit to listening and responding to what you hear, as opposed to what you *expect* to hear or what you believe you *should* hear.
- Don't be tempted to use this tool merely to pretend to be a more compassionate, caring, and responsive leader than you really are. Employees will see through the ruse immediately.

- Be sensitive to the unintentional messages you may send to those whom you choose *not* to interview. They see being left out as a sign of their unimportance. Your interviewee selection should be "organizationally correct" in terms of both the formal and the informal organizational structure. Don't cause hard feelings.
- Avoid information overload by conducting no more than three or four interviews a day.

4 TOOLS FOR TEAMWORK

Team Builder

Resources needed:

Flip charts with markers
Post-it notes
¾-inch colored sticky dots
Meeting room

Tools to consult:

Meeting Leader

What Problems Does Team Builder Solve?

- Team members aren't on the same wavelength; they don't mesh as they should.
- We have an important task ahead that we won't achieve unless we all work together as a unit.

What Is the Aim of This Tool?

As he signed the Declaration of Independence, Benjamin Franklin supposedly looked up at his fellow patriots and said, "We must all hang together or most assuredly we shall all hang separately." The purpose of Team Builder is to determine how well your team is hanging together and to pinpoint what you can do to keep its members from hanging separately.

Through Team Builder your team will compare its behavior to a profile of ideal team behavior. Based on the resulting data, the team will devise a strategy to strengthen its cohesiveness and thereby magnify its productivity.

Team Builder is designed principally to improve the health and vitality of an existing team; however, with certain modifications it can also serve a new team well in the early stages of its existence.

How Does Team Builder Work?

Team Builder can be conducted in six hours or less and can accommodate a team with up to 30 members. Someone other than a team member should conduct the retreat. Use either a professional facilitator or someone in your company who has no immediate vested interest in the outcome of the team's work and has group facilitation skills.

This tool provides an intensive, highly structured format in which a team can critically assess its strengths and weaknesses. On the basis of that assessment, the group devises action plans for increasing its cohesiveness and effectiveness.

The steps outlined represent the typical format for conducting the team-building session; however, you should feel free to customize the materials to meet the unique needs of your group.

Step 1: Have everyone take the "Team Test."

The "Team Test" on page 62 is an exercise to see how well the team meets the 22 criteria of effective teams. Team members will use one of six response options to indicate the level of their agreement with 22 statements.

You may want to add items to the Team Test to measure other dimensions of team play important to your group, and you may choose to remove some items that are not relevant.

Step 2: Celebrate team strengths.

Congratulate team members on the 4s and the 5s on their tests. Lead a discussion of which of the highly scored items contributes the most to team success.

In order to carry out Step 2 and future steps it will be useful to have a profile of team members' ratings visible in the front of the room. First, give each participant a sheet of colored sticky dots. Draw a chart on two sheets of large flip-chart paper containing a box for each of the 22 statements, much like the one below. After doing the test, participants can for each statement put sticky dots in the correct cell. This will create a graphic display of the

Statement	5	4	3	2	1	0
1. Common vision						
2. Consistent core values						
3. . . .						

Team Test

5 : Strongly agree 4 : Agree 3 : Slightly agree 2 : Slightly disagree 1 : Disagree 0 : Strongly disagree

___ 1. We share a common vision. We're all heading in the direction of the same dream, future, and aspiration.

___ 2. We share consistent core values and beliefs about what is important for this team.

___ 3. New members added to this team come with the ability and the motivation to perform effectively for us.

___ 4. We trust each other's motives and accept behavior we don't immediately understand.

___ 5. We defend, support, and speak well of each other.

___ 6. We enjoy each other's company and have fun together.

___ 7. We share our ideas, opinions, and feelings openly and honestly.

___ 8. We speak our minds without attacking, feeling attacked, or getting in trouble for our honesty.

___ 9. We welcome disagreement and diversity of opinion.

___ 10. We listen to each other.

___ 11. We give each other honest and constructive criticism.

___ 12. We give each other abundant and uplifting credit and praise.

___ 13. We treat each other with courtesy and respect.

___ 14. We turn to each other for advice and help, and it's given freely.

___ 15. We challenge each other's thinking in order to avoid "group-think."

___ 16. We uniformly support team decisions, even after stating our concerns with them to the team.

___ 17. Our meetings are great: they start and end on time, they're well attended, they stay on track, people contribute equally and constructively, and we get things done.

___ 18. We give each other the information and other resources we need to do our jobs.

___ 19. We give each other clear statements of our performance expectations of each other.

___ 20. We meet each other's expectations fully, and we are accountable to each other.

___ 21. We follow through on the promises we make to each other.

___ 22. I believe that the members of this team are genuinely interested in seeing the team, and not just themselves or their special interests, succeed.

scores: the more dots are clustered to the left, the better. The Step 2 discussion can be accomplished in 10 to 15 minutes.

Step 3: Set goals for team development.

Encourage the team to select five low-ranked items as goals for team development. Then give each team member a pad of 3×5-inch Post-it notes and have them write as many from-to statements as they wish for the targeted items. For instance, for item #1 a team member might write, "*From* different views of our future *to* a widely shared aspiration." They may need 15 to 20 minutes for this.

Post the from-to statements on large sheets of flip-chart paper headed by titles corresponding to the items selected for team development. Give members ten minutes to mill around in front of the sheets to get a sense of how their colleagues want to improve the team.

Depending on the size of the group, assign a subgroup to each sheet (or as many as two sheets) to study the Post-It notes on the sheet and to emerge with one or two consensus from-to statements that appear to reflect the will of the team. Allow 30 to 60 minutes for this task, depending upon the number of sheets assigned to each subgroup as well as the number of Post-it notes they need to synthesize.

Have each group make a five-minute presentation on its consensus from-to statements. Give members the opportunity to comment on how well they believe the consensus from-to statements presented by the subgroups reflect the concerns measured by the Team Test. Revise the from-to statements accordingly. Aim to come out of this process with no more than eight to ten from-to statements posted on a single flip-chart sheet in the front of the room.

Reassemble the whole team. Issue three sticky dots to each team member. With a felt-tip marker make a black circle in the center of one of the three dots. Ask team members to designate on the flip-chart sheet which three of the eight to ten from-to statements they believe are most vital to the team, using the dot with the black center to indicate their top choice. Count the dots, assigning two points to the black-center dots and one point to all others, to determine the priority of the from-to statements. This will take no more than ten minutes to perform and discuss.

Step 4: Analyze the goals.

Lead the team through a force-field analysis of the from-to statements, beginning with the highest-ranked statement, to contrast the forces that have been operating in support of the from-to with the restraining forces, which operate against it. The rationale of the force-field analysis is that the from-to will be attained by a combination of reinforcing the supporting forces and countering the restraining ones. For this purpose use a flip-chart sheet format like the one below.

From Different Views of the Future
to a Widely Shared Aspiration

Supporting Forces ⇒	⇐ Restraining Forces
Our team understands and accepts the need for a well-defined vision.	We have never developed a formal vision statement.
⋮	⋮

Keep the discussion on track. Resist the tendency of team members to jump ahead to propose actions to counter the restraining forces. Allow 15 to 20 minutes for each force field. Once you've done two or three force fields, expect to find that you can eliminate some as a result of duplication.

Step 5: Fix the future.

Post the flip-chart sheets containing the force-field analyses in full view from left to right according to the priority of the from-to statements they address. Lead the team through an examination of the entries in the force fields. What actions do these entries indicate the team can take to increase its effectiveness? On flip-chart sheets, list them in the left-hand column as shown on page 65.

Most teams spend 60 to 90 minutes on this activity and end up with three to ten actions. One way to assign responsibilities in the "Who?" column is to instruct team members to print their names on sticky dots for every action plan ("What?") they would like to contribute to. (Each person should be expected to contribute to at least one action plan.) Once everyone has placed their dots next to

"Fix the Future" Chart

What Action to Take	Who?	When?
Plan a three-hour work session to create a vision statement.	John Jane	By 3/30
⋮	⋮	⋮

the action plans they will work on, ask for volunteers to head up each action plan and get agreement on the dates ("When?") they will complete the actions.

Step 6: Establish accountability.

The entire team should reconvene with the facilitator in about eight weeks to assess progress. In the meantime, how will you ensure that the action groups follow through on their assignments? You might set aside time at staff meetings to review progress on the action plans, or you might convene a special action plan review committee.

How Do I Make Team Builder Work for Me?

One way to administer the Team Test is to allow group members to rate the items without any assistance in interpreting them. Alternatively, if the facilitator has a good grasp of the issues represented by the statements, he or she can comment on the contribution of each item to group health as participants rate them item by item. The first method will take less than 15 minutes; the second method will take anywhere from 15 to 60 minutes, depending upon the depth of discussion by the facilitator.

A typical Team Builder agenda is shown on page 66.

Modifications to Team Builder for Newly Formed Teams

With these modifications you can use Team Builder to launch a new team in the right direction:

1. Eliminate the six-level rating scale in the Team Test. Replace the blank line in front of each survey item with a smiling and a frowning face. Rephrase the survey items to reflect desired future states for the team. For example, "1. We will share a

common vision. We'll all head in the direction of the same dream, future, and aspiration."

2. Change the directions for the survey to read: "Which *seven* team factors described below will be *most* vital to the success of the team? Indicate these by circling the smiling face in front of their description. Similarly, circle the frowning faces in front of the *seven* items that you believe are *least* vital."
3. On the basis of the group count of smiles and frowns, help the team choose the seven or so items that they predict will be most vital for team success. Next have them use the six-level scale to indicate their level of agreement that each of the chosen team factors will come about without any special effort or advance planning.
4. For the lowest-scored of the seven team factors, take the team through force-field analyses and action planning.

Typical Team Builder Agenda

9:00–9:30 A.M.	Have them take the Team Test. (Step 1)
9:30–9:45 A.M.	Celebrate team strengths. (Step 2)
9:45–10:15 A.M.	Set goals for team development. (Step 3)
10:15–10:30 A.M.	Break.
10:30 A.M.–Noon	Analyze the goals. (Step 4)
Noon–1:00 P.M.—	Lunch.
1:00–2:30 P.M.	Analyze the goals (cont.).
2:30–3:50 P.M.	Fix the future. (Step 5)
3:50–4:00 P.M.	Establish accountability. (Step 6)

Team Links

Resources needed:

None

Tools to consult:

Team Builder
Customer Focus
Performance Pay

What Problems Does Team Links Solve?

- We need more teamwork in this company, from top to bottom.
- We need better communication throughout the company.
- We serve external clients fairly well, but internal customer service is dreadful.

What Is the Aim of This Tool?

What number on a scale from 0 to 10 would you use to rate the quality of service your employees provide to your external customers, the ultimate consumers of your products or services? If you're like most managers, you'll answer somewhere in the range of 7 to 9.

How would you rate the quality of service your employees provide to each other, their internal customers? If you're like most managers, your rating will be in the range of 3 to 5.

One final question: What is one of the surest ways to raise your 7–9 rating to a 10? Maybe you guessed it—by raising that 3, 4, or 5 to a higher figure. In other words, in most companies the quality of *external* customer service is dependent on the quality of *internal* customer service.

The purpose of Team Links is to enable your company to improve the satisfaction received by your external customers by improving the satisfaction your employees provide to their internal customers: team members and peers, counterparts in other departments, and colleagues who depend on the in-company services other employees and departments provide.

How Does Team Links Work?

Managers who rate their internal customer service higher than the typical 3–5 range work in organizations where teams, departments, and divisions do an excellent job of meeting the requirements they have of each other. That's the key: fulfillment of expectations.

Here's what you can do to ensure that your teams, departments, and divisions feel accountable for meeting each other's expectations.

Step 1: Create a rating instrument.

Put a survey instrument together that enables each one of your departments (e.g., marketing) to assess the service provided to it by all other departments (e.g., finance, engineering, manufacturing, sales, and personnel). Your actual survey will, of course, contain those items that are relevant to your operation. You might call it an "Interdepartmental Service Survey," and it might look and read something like the sample below.

Sample Interdepartmental Service Survey

Use the scale below to rate the quality of service you believe your department receives from each of the departments listed in the chart. Write "NA" if the item is not applicable to your relationship with that department. Leave all the boxes blank under your own department.

5 : Strongly agree 4 : Agree 3 : Slightly agree
2 : Slightly disagree 1 : Disagree 0 : Strongly disagree

	Marketing	Finance	Engineering	Manufacturing	Sales	Personnel
1. Understands our mission and goals.						
2. Respects our mission and goals.						
3. Has made its mission and goals clear to us.						

4. Has made its needs and expectations clear to us.						
5. Makes reasonable requests.						
6. Responds quickly to our requests.						
7. Treats our employees with respect.						
8. Works collaboratively, not competitively.						
9. Gives us timely information; keeps us informed.						
10. Has employees knowledgeable in their fields.						
11. Is committed to excellence and total quality.						
12. Follows through on commitments to us.						
13. Is open to criticism.						
14. Takes a problem-solving approach to disputes we have with them.						

Step 2: Decide who should participate in the survey.

Include all departments. Depending on the situation in your company, you might have only department heads perform the ratings. Alternatively, you might choose to include either a select group of employees or all employees who work in the departments, depending on the value you believe their ratings will add to the survey.

Step 3: Administer the survey and analyze results.

Select a time that least disrupts your organization's operations. Get the survey out and back quickly. Calculate the average score attained by each department on each service item.

Step 4: Report results.

Reveal the results at a meeting with your employees, but do not publish them in a hard-copy format that might sprout legs and walk out of the building. The power of this survey is that it bares all; that baring should stay in the corporate family.

Step 5: Reward employees of highest-scoring departments.

Create plaques for each department that scored highest on at least one survey item. Reserve the fanciest plaque for the "Department of the Year," the one that scores highest overall. If possible, provide employees of this department with a financial bonus. (See *Performance Pay*.)

Step 6: Demand improvement from the lowest-scoring departments.

Insist on a written plan for improvement from each department that scores near the bottom on any of the survey items. An even more comprehensive blueprint for future success should be required of the departments that score near the bottom of the ratings overall. Department heads of chronically low-scoring departments should be censured. Be sure, however, to remain sensitive to the possibility that some departments by virtue of their function might receive artificially inflated or deflated scores on the survey. For instance, finance departments might be expected to be underrated on the item "Makes reasonable requests."

Step 7: Look for friction between two departments.

Survey results may uncover service problems and even antagonisms between particular departments. If so, address these "relationships in need." If conflict resolution is in order, provide it. If counseling is in order, provide that.

It is unlikely that the heads of two warring departments will communicate well with each other. A tool like *Team Builder* focusing on the senior staff might be one of your best sources of interdepartmental harmony.

There are three main reasons, in addition to friction between department heads, why departments fail to serve each other well:

1. The employees in each department may not understand or appreciate the work of the other.

2. The employees in each department may not know exactly what those in the other(s) require from them.
3. Good internal customer service may not be rewarded from the top, and poor internal customer service may not bring consequences from the top.

Counteract these three negative factors in these ways:

- Give your employees tours of the entire company operation; give them cross-training; have them spend one day working beside a counterpart from another department; have departments host groups from other departments for briefings of what they do.
- Get departments to share written lists of the expectations they have of each other, have them negotiate and discuss their lists, and provide opportunities for periodic updates.
- See that great internal customer service is praised and rewarded; censure anything less.

How Do I Make Team Links Work for Me?

- Team Links will have maximum impact when you put more energy into celebrating the departments that serve each other well than you put into chastising those who don't.
- Give the departments ownership of this tool. Let them select the items that will appear on the survey and appoint a group who will tally the results. Get them to choose who will complete the survey. Have them suggest the rewards and the corrections that will be dispensed to the winners and losers. Ask them to pick a snappy name for the tool.
- Monitor the progress of Team Links to ensure that it does not in any way become a destructively competitive factor in the relationships among your departments.

Meeting Leader

Resources needed:

None

Tools to consult:

Team Builder
Fight Right
Criticism Template

What Problems Does Meeting Leader Solve?

- I'm not satisfied with my ability to run effective meetings.
- We're not very effective at group problem solving.
- How can I get people to share their ideas openly and honestly in meetings?

What Is the Aim of This Tool?

You've probably heard that meetings are a place where people take minutes and waste hours. That a committee of three gets things done if two people don't show up. That if God had sent the Israelites a committee instead of Moses they would still be in Egypt.

Unfortunately, these sayings are often too near to the truth in many organizations. We conduct a lot of our business and make significant decisions in group meetings. Yet very few of these gatherings satisfy the people who attend them. Why? Because so few of them are chaired by leaders who know how to run an efficient and effective meeting.

This tool can put an end to frustrating meetings in your company. It shows the heads of task forces, committees, focus groups, and staff meetings how to conduct a meeting where the right things get done. Even the members of self-directed teams will profit from learning what responsibilities they must all share for an effective group process.

How Does Meeting Leader Work?

Every meeting needs a dictator! Before you condemn that statement as being too harsh, consider what it really means.

There are two dimensions to any meeting: the *process* and the *content.* The content is the agenda, the points that are raised, and the decisions that are made. The content is the "what" of the meeting. The process is the "how" of the meeting. The process includes how well the plan of the agenda is followed, the quality of communication, the way in which disagreement is resolved, and other interpersonal dynamics of the meeting. When we call for a meeting dictator, we mean a *process* dictator: someone who will keep the meeting on track and see to it that group members are making the best possible use of themselves. The process dictator can be the group leader, or it can be all members of the group, who mutually pledge themselves to rule over the process.

The best group leader keeps a heavy hand on the conduct of the meeting but has the lightest touch regarding the content. As much as possible, this person follows the central spirit of *Robert's Rules of Order,* the internationally recognized standard book of instructions for the proper (parliamentary) conduct of meetings. *Robert's* forces the chair to control the *process* and disallows the chair from making any sort of *content* input without first relinquishing the chair.

Step 1: Take the "Meeting Leader Inventory" test of group discussion leadership.

Mark each statement on the inventory on pages 74–75 with the appropriate rating. If your team functions without one person in charge, (a "self-directed team"), reword the statements as necessary to reflect *group* responsibility whenever the pronoun "I" is used.

Step 2: Score the "Meeting Leader Inventory."

Circle all scores higher than 3. Congratulations on these. They are evidence of effective group leadership, which your team most certainly appreciates. Study your lower scores. Which of these represent the best targets of opportunity for you to improve the success of the meetings you run? Is there anyone who can help you on these by giving you additional feedback? Is there anyone on the team who can help you on these by assuming part of the responsibility to make sure these lower-scored items get turned around?

Meeting Leader Inventory

5 : Almost always 4 : Often 3 : Sometimes
2 : Infrequently 1 : Rarely 0 : Never

Before our meetings . . .

____ 1. An agenda is prepared and circulated specifying date, place, starting and ending times, purpose, attendees, and topics to be discussed.

____ 2. All support materials such as audiovisual equipment, extra agendas, background material, flip chart and markers, and refreshments are on hand.

Early in the group's life . . .

____ 3. Members discuss and agree upon a precise set of expectations for their behavior, including attendance, punctuality, contribution, and all aspects of their participation in the meetings.

____ 4. I elicit from them a precise set of expectations for how they need me to function as the group leader in order for them to succeed.

At the beginning of our meetings . . .

____ 5. I introduce those who are new to the group and ask veteran members to describe our team and what we have accomplished recently.

____ 6. The first order of business is to review the agenda and the goals of the meeting and to state those goals in terms of the specific outcomes we're shooting for.

As the meeting proceeds . . .

____ 7. When members appear not to understand or listen to each other I point this out to them.

____ 8. When conflict, disagreement, or personal antagonisms block progress, I make sure the issues are confronted honestly, yet tactfully, and the dispute is resolved directly.

____ 9. Whenever discussion strays from the agenda, I focus us back to the topic at hand.

____ 10. I ensure that once we make appropriate progress on an agenda item we move on to the next one without undue delay.

____ 11. I avoid "group-think." When group members agree too quickly, without thoroughly assessing their assumptions and assertions, I lead them through a more critical evaluation of their ideas. So as not to risk making a group-think decision, I force them to ask, "What might go wrong with this plan?"

___ 12. I draw noncontributing members into the discussion without embarrassing them.
___ 13. When the group is making good progress, I spend far more time listening than speaking.
___ 14. When any group member makes an assertion that is either vital to the team or to that member, I make certain that at least one other person comments on it before we move on. I don't allow us to engage in a series of disassociated monologues, except when brainstorming.
___ 15. On a regular basis, I suspend our work on the agenda (the "content") so we can examine the health of our *process* and take necessary steps to improve it.
___ 16. When I or team members criticize people's ideas or their violations of team expectations, I make sure that criticism is constructive.
___ 17. Every 90 minutes, or sooner if energy wanes, I call for a break.

Before the meeting ends . . .

___ 18. I thank, recognize, and praise team members for their contributions to the group effort.
___ 19. I lead a summary of the decisions we've made and remind members of whatever follow-up tasks they have agreed to perform for the group.

After the meeting . . .

___ 20. I send reminders to members regarding whatever follow-up tasks they have agreed to perform for the group.
___ 21. I speak confidentially to any members whose behavior in meetings is counterproductive.

Step 3: Consider inventory item #3 above.

Few meeting leaders are able to score their teams high on this item: "Members discuss and agree upon a precise set of expectations for their behavior, including attendance, punctuality, contribution, and all aspects of their participation in the meetings."

One of us was asked to chair a communitywide task force to improve relations between the school district and several community organizations. The task force was made up of 32 community leaders from nearly every political, fraternal, educational, and public-service organization. Anticipating the difficulties of keeping that group on track, the chairman showed up at the first meeting with the memo printed on the following page.

TO: The Task Force
FROM: Your Chairman
RE: The Good, the Bad, and the Ugly

When a group meets to achieve a common goal, certain behaviors help and others hurt. We might call these the "good," the "bad," and the "ugly." The *good* are the behaviors we need on this team. The more you do these, the more successful we will be. The *bad* are those unfortunate things that occur at meetings. When they impede progress, my job is to point them out and call for their elimination. Any *ugly* is unacceptable behavior, given the importance of our task. One *ugly* and you're off the task force.

The Good

1. Arrive on time.
2. Come prepared, having read the agenda and having done your homework.
3. Listen to others; make sure you understand what they say.
4. Speak to contribute to the goals of the task force, rather than speaking just to hear yourself talk or to further one of your causes.
5. Build on the present discussion; don't change the focus to suit your own goals.
6. Maintain a problem-solving focus, not a blame-placing attitude.
7. Remain upbeat. Focus on what we *can* do, rather than agonize over what we *cannot* do.
8. Challenge bad ideas; don't let us get away with sloppy thinking.
9. Help me. When I miss something that I should address as the meeting leader, call me on it.
10. Remain fiercely dedicated to our goals.

The Bad

1. Miss meetings without letting us know in advance.
2. Wait until the meeting ends to share your attitudes, opinions, and ideas privately with another task force member.
3. Ignore the agenda, and take the discussion in the direction you want it to go.
4. Monopolize discussions or elaborate unnecessarily on your ideas.
5. Continue to dredge up the past when our need is to focus on the future and solve a problem.
6. Criticize task force members, instead of criticizing their ideas.

7. React defensively to well-intentioned criticisms of your ideas.
8. Do other work or daydream during meetings.
9. Fail to return on time after breaks.
10. Allow your beeper to go off or your cell telephone to ring during a meeting.

The Ugly

1. Use this group as a forum in which to launch agendas for personal gain.
2. Intentionally withhold information we need to solve a particular problem.
3. Leak confidential discussions.
4. Criticize this task force to outsiders.
5. Show disrespect or contempt for another member during a meeting.
6. Fail to support the implementation of task force decisions.
7. Speak to the media without checking with me first.

Consider how you might use a communication like the memo to get your group started on the right track. The expectations you state in each category will differ depending on the makeup of the team and its purpose. This approach to creating team member expectations might be even more effective if you explain the three categories of behaviors to the team and have *them* draft the behaviors that fit into each category.

How Do I Make Meeting Leader Work for Me?

- Have others (perhaps the whole team) complete the Meeting Leader Inventory for you so you can compare their feedback with yours. Instead of having them use the rating scale, it may be better to have them pick three of the items they believe you practice most consistently and three that they believe you practice least consistently. (See *Lemons and Oranges.*)
- Ask your team to tell you which of the 21 group leadership behaviors they believe are most crucial for the success of the team. This is one way to accomplish item #4 on the Meeting Leader Inventory.
- Without having them rate you with the inventory, simply go to your team with the scores you gave yourself. Ask them if they feel you rated yourself accurately, and ask them for any ideas they may have on how you can improve.

- Share the Meeting Leader Inventory with other meeting leaders who can benefit from reviewing their leadership behavior. Use the Meeting Leader Inventory as the outline for a training curriculum for the meeting leaders in your organization.

Resources needed:

None

Tools to consult:

Hero Table
Team Builder

Players On the Bench

What Problems Does Players On the Bench Solve?

- How do I give recognition to our support staff and our unsung heroes?
- We need more teamwork in this company—from top to bottom.

What Is the Aim of This Tool?

The purpose of this tool is to identify team members who have yet to receive the accolades they deserve. In any organization, certain employees will have greater power, prestige, and status than others. The difference might be attributed to differences in salary, visibility of the specific job, or both. Regardless of why the difference exists, management must walk the talk of teamwork. Companies where stars are rewarded while support staff feel neglected are companies where teamwork is seen by many as a hollow platitude and a manipulative ploy. Unless management acknowledges the value of a tool such as Players On the Bench, morale problems will be a precursor to lower productivity and lost income.

Every company today preaches teamwork, and the metaphors used are often borrowed from sports. In fact some of the most popular speakers at corporate team-building conferences are professional sports stars, Olympic champions, and coaches. The sports metaphor has obvious power and implications for companies "fighting" for market share, "scoring points" against the competition, and shooting for the "slam dunk," "hole in one," "hat trick," or "home run."

Unfortunately, a fixation with sports metaphors and star athletes at company retreats causes us to lose sight of the crucial role played by utility players and bench warmers. Second-stringers never make the cover of *Sports Illustrated* or have their picture on a box of Wheaties. They never sign lucrative cologne contracts or have candy bars named after them. In the same way, support staff in companies seldom receive the same recognition as star salespeople or top-producing divisional managers.

Yet without second-stringers there would be no championship teams. Without bench warmers to practice against, the starting team would not be as competitive. Without reserve players to relieve starting players, stars would be too exhausted to compete. Without sturdy blockers, star halfbacks would have no room to run. Players On the Bench helps you avoid the fatal error of rewarding only those who make the corporate headlines. It recognizes those who enable your stars to shine so the team can win.

How Does Players On the Bench Work?

Players On the Bench yields a yearly award given to employees who demonstrate the best qualities of teamwork. The award is based on companywide nominations. See the sample announcement soliciting nominations on pages 82–83.

Step 1: Obtain nominations for team players of the year from your employees.

In a small company where everyone knows the work of everyone else, the voting can be companywide. In larger companies, you may want to have people nominate candidates within their plant, division, or department.

Step 2: Collect ballots and announce winners.

Give the awards at a companywide meeting. The award will be doubly appreciated if recipients hear and see the adulation from the rest of the team. You may even want to schedule a special awards dinner to which family members of winners are invited and are also given awards. This sends a powerful message that they are part of the team and that their support of their loved one is recognized and appreciated.

How Do I Make Players On the Bench Work for Me?

Create your own metaphors for winning categories.

We recognize that in some workplaces a sports metaphor will be more confusing than motivating or will even turn people off. Think of other metaphors instead. For instance the theater: Who is your stage manager, ensuring everything runs smoothly behind the scenes? Your lighting director, who makes people look good? Your ticket seller, who is the first person customers meet?

Decide on the timing for awards.

You might want the voting to take place yearly for all categories. Alternatively, you could give awards every month, every two months, or every quarter for just one or two categories.

Talk about Team Player Awards at new-employee orientation.

Create a culture of teams and teamwork with every new employee you hire. Defining the roles of cheerleader, assist leader, trainer, lead blocker, and comeback kid gives new employees concrete examples of the behavior you're looking for. Focusing their attention on the Rookie of the Year Award gives them something even more tangible to shoot for.

Acknowledge all nominees.

When you announce the winners, also provide a listing of all employees who received at least one vote for one of the categories. This would be a nice summary to publish in a company newsletter. Also send a personal note of thanks to each person on the list.

Ask your fans to vote for their favorite players.

Your fans are your customers and your suppliers. Send a letter asking them to nominate any of your employees who have gone "above and beyond" to satisfy them. Keep it simple. You'll get names of truck drivers, clerks, warehouse workers, and other support staff who might otherwise remain anonymous. You'll strengthen bonds with customers and suppliers as well as with your employees.

We're Looking for Team Stars

We're always preaching teamwork at [name of company]. Now we're doing more than preaching. We're going to reward team players who are essential for team success.

Please nominate seven of your coworkers for our "Team Player" Awards. Read the description for each award and write in the name of the person who best fits that description. Every person who receives even one nomination in a category will be acknowledged; the recipient of the most nominations will get a well-deserved award.

Thank you, and "Go team!!"

Our Cheerleader

Who on our team lifts the spirit, turns clouds into sunshine and lemons into lemonade? Who consistently roots for our team, even though he or she may not always get the glory? Who improves our performance with a smile on his or her face, a pep talk when we need it most, and a spark of inspiration? Who gets your vote for Cheerleader of the Year? ____________

Our Assist Leader

The Great Gretzky not only scores, he also passes the puck. Michael Jordan not only dazzles with dunks, he also passes the ball. Great teams are great not because of star players but because of unselfish players. Who on our team can most often be counted on to fill in capably when someone is sick? Who consistently will do whatever the team asks, even if it's not in the job description? Who is always looking for ways to pitch in to help the team? Who gets your vote for Assist Leader of the Year? ____________

Our Trainer

A trainer on a sports team makes sure that players are physically fit and ready to play. The trainer dispenses bandages, aspirin, whirlpool treatments, and advice in game-saving quantities. Who is the trainer on your team? Who listens when people are down; who cares about their well being and always seems to know the right thing to say to help others heal? Who makes sure team members are emotionally ready to play? Who gets your vote for Trainer of the Year? ____________

Our Lead Blocker

If you could consistently gain over a thousand yards a year on a professional football team, your annual compensation might be in eight figures. On each of your runs you'd be depending on a lineman—a lead blocker—to clear a safe path for your journey toward the end zone. If that blocking deteriorated such than your average yardage per run dropped by as little as 25 percent, your team would suffer dramatically, and you might go from an eight-figure salary to free agent status. Our company also can't succeed without reliable lead blockers. Who does the most to clear the way for others? Who does the best job of making team members look good? Who works hard to make others succeed without getting his or her name in lights? Who gets your vote for Lead Blocker of the Year? ______________

Our Comeback Kid

Have you ever noticed that champions often emerge from adversity? Dan Jensen, the Olympic skater, won his gold medal after several bad breaks and heartbreaking defeats. Rocky Blier, star running back for the Pittsburgh Steelers during the seventies, was wounded in Vietnam and told he would never be able to play football again. Kerri Strug helped the 1996 U.S. women's gymnastic team win a gold medal by "sticking" her final vault in spite of a severely bruised ankle. We have a Dan Jensen, Rocky Bleier, or Kerri Strug on our team. Who is it? Who on our team came back from adversity, proving to us all that winners never lose and losers never win? Who gets your vote for Comeback Kid of the Year? ______________

Our Most Improved Player

Sports teams give awards to players who show the most improvement over the previous year. They are examples to their teammates and prove the adage that it's not important where you start but where you finally end up. Who has done the most to improve their skills and their performance? Which member on your team continues to learn from experience? Who gets your vote for Most Improved Player of the Year? ______________

Our Rookie of the Year

Every major professional sport honors a freshman player who has shown potential to be a league star. Which employee who has joined us sometime in the past 12 months has all the earmarks of a future star? Who among our "freshmen" is quickly becoming indispensable to our team? Who through effort, commitment, and performance has been impressing us since day one? Who gets your vote for Rookie of the Year? ______________

Fight Right

Resources needed:

None

Tools to consult:

Frame It
Gripe Session
Criticism Template

What Problems Does Fight Right Solve?

- I need to improve my conflict-resolution skills.
- There's a person I'm having a lot of trouble dealing with.

What Is the Aim of This Tool?

In our world people appear to be getting less tolerant of each other's behavior and more willing to put up their dukes at the slightest provocation. You see it in families, you see it at sporting events, you see it at the teller's window, you see it on the shop floor, you see it on the highway, you see it in the classroom, and you even see it in the corporate boardroom. In these troubled times it is important for you to know how to work through your disagreements with others so that they are resolved with a minimum of rancor and a maximum of satisfaction for both of you.

Many disagreements, because of the poor way they are handled, end up in win-lose or lose-lose results. Sometimes one person comes out on top of the other; other times, two combatants come out of a battle with less than they started with. Fight Right reveals the essential actions that will help you achieve win-win outcomes in your arguments with others.

How Does Fight Right Work?

Fight Right identifies 11 conflict-resolution behaviors. In order to be able to practice these behaviors consistently, you need to know how well you do with each of them. Once you know how fully you practice each one, you can focus your energies on those that are weak or lacking in your conflict-resolution repertoire.

Step 1: Take the "Conflict-Resolution Survey."

Try to recall the typical interactions you have with a particular person when the two of you disagree. Use the survey below to improve your conflict-resolution skills by indicating how you behave

Conflict-Resolution Survey

5 : Almost always 4 : Often 3 : Sometimes 2 : Infrequently 1 : Rarely 0 : Never

___ 1. When I disagree, I am honest about the fact that I disagree, and why.

___ 2. When proven wrong, I admit it, rather than deny it or try to cover my tracks.

___ 3. In our oral exchanges I let the other person talk first; I don't have to get in my two cents' worth before he or she speaks.

___ 4. Before I respond to the other person's assertions, I ask questions or attempt to paraphrase his or her points to make certain I understand what was said.

___ 5. I stay calm and rational, being careful not to engage in name-calling or to otherwise say anything I'll regret later.

___ 6. When I do allow myself to get angry, I talk about that anger, rather than what the person did to elicit it.

___ 7. I am careful to direct my attacks at issues, not personalities. I condemn this person's claims without condemning him or her for making them.

___ 8. Even as I may disagree with the person's assertions, I recognize the validity of his or her feelings.

___ 9. I direct our attention to *fixing the future* rather than rehashing the past.

___ 10. I keep the focus on our comparative needs, *not our opposing positions,* so we can search for creative ways to meet both sets of needs and reach a common ground.

___ 11. I use *we, us,* and *our,* rather than *I, me,* and *you* when discussing the issue.

with the person you have identified. The more honest you can be on the survey, the more valuable it will be to you.

Step 2: Circle all scores below a 4.

Are these items more a reflection of your relationship with this particular person or more a reflection of your personal conflict-resolution style? One way to answer this question is to complete the survey for other people in your life with whom you have disagreements. Note which items tend to be scored differently—a reflection of the relationship—and which remain unchanged—your conflict-resolution style. What do these scores suggest you do differently the next time you come into conflict with this person or someone else?

Step 3: Choose the new conflict-resolution behaviors you will adopt.

These recommended improvements in problem-solving skills are keyed by number to the items in the survey.

1. Honesty. When you disagree with someone, what is the trigger that brings your disagreement into discussion? Is it because you say something like, "We have a problem"? Or does the discussion begin only after the person notices you acting strangely and calls you on it? Do you admit your disagreement, or do you sulk? When you have something to say but you choose not to, you engage in a form of passive-aggressive behavior. You are being unfair to the other person, to your team, and to yourself.

2. "I was wrong." Many people foolishly believe that admitting error is a sign of weakness that will compromise their position in a disagreement. Quite the opposite is true. When you admit to having been wrong about something, you are in the best position to ask other people to reciprocate in some way. You might ask them to make a similar admission about one of their previous assertions or actions. An admission of blame, liability, or error gives you an excellent excuse to ask others for a concession in their position. Admitting wrong also happens to be the right thing to do.

3. Speak second. In an argument it is foolish to go first and smart to go second for at least four reasons. First, letting other people "get it all out" will help to calm them down and defuse their anger. Second, your willingness to wait is a sign of respect that they will appreciate. Third, by listening carefully to their assertions, you will gain clues to what it will take to persuade them over to your way of thinking. (That's why someone once said, "The second lie always wins.") Finally, and most important, only after others have emptied themselves of their ideas, emotions, and anger are they likely to pay much attention to yours.

4. Make sure you understand. The single greatest cause of interpersonal conflict is little more than misunderstanding. Don't take a chance that miscommunication is at the root of a disagreement you have with someone. Ask clarifying questions before you put your foot into your mouth. When possible encourage the playing of the "paraphrasing game." The first person starts by stating his or her position. The second person must paraphrase to the first person's satisfaction what he or she just said before earning the right to respond. Continue the entire conversation in this manner with permission to talk always tied to a successful paraphrase. You'll be amazed at the results!

5. Bite your tongue. A number of years ago, 100 people aged 95 and older were asked the question "If you could live your life over again, what would you do differently?" The most frequent response they gave was that they would have thought longer before they did and said to others some of the stupid things they did and said. In other words, they realized that three things in life cannot be recalled: time passed, the spent arrow, and the spoken word. If in anger you tell people you'll never trust them again, you might forget what you said when you calm down. They may never forget. You painful words will haunt your relationship for many years. Talk is cheap, but you can't buy it back.

6. Talk about your anger. Much of the advice in the survey is intended to limit your anger. When that advice doesn't work and you lose your temper, start immediately to talk about it. Describe your emotions, your pain, your fear. Only when you have vented completely should you then talk about the incident you got angry about. *Never* talk about what the person did to make you angry, because that would be a lie. People don't have the ability to make you angry without your full cooperation.

7. Condemn claims, not claimers. Attack issues with full force, while letting people escape unscathed. Don't accuse others of a dishonest intent. They'll never see it that way and therefore will conclude that you are malicious. Instead, pinpoint the behavior or the issue and state what your needs are in regard to it. Example: Instead of labeling a devious colleague a "backstabber," describe the unacceptable behavior you observe and insist upon something better.

8. Allow for feelings. All feelings are valid. They are part of our human nature and are not contrived. We should never say something inappropriate like "You have no right to feel that way." Some people have a powerful need to discuss their feelings as a prelude to resolving the conflict into which those feelings are woven. Give them every opportunity to do that even if you don't share that need. You will increase your chances for a win-win outcome.

9. Fix the future. Why do we resolve conflict? To prevent more of the same in the future. The ideal posture to take with regard to your antagonists is best described by the question "What can we do to keep this from happening again?" At some point two people in conflict need to stop talking about the behavior that has contributed to the clash and even stop talking about the feelings that have resulted. One trick for getting the two of you on track to a solution is to invoke the "30-minute rule." It works like this: "Let's agree that for the rest of this discussion neither one of us will talk about anything that happened more than a half hour ago."

10. Meet needs; don't take positions. Two people in a disagreement often take opposite positions on an issue. As the debate flares, they harden their stances. This approach leaves little in the way of resolution possibilities other than compromise. A fragile peace is won only after both sides are willing to retreat from their positions to a middle ground that neither side likes, but both realize they must accept. A more satisfying outcome for both parties is possible when they define their differences in terms of needs, not positions. When each person has the opportunity to say, "This is what I want to accomplish by taking this position, or these are the values and beliefs I have that lead me to this conclusion," the two of you can engage in problem solving. You become capable of searching for a new alternative—one that meets the needs of both of you—that neither of you previously considered because of the hardness of your positions. And so you're both happy because the underlying needs that caused you to assume apparently irreconcilable positions are met.

11. Favor cooperative pronouns. Pronouns like "I," "me," and "mine" represent the language of a position taker. Pronouns like "we," "our," and "us" encourage collaboration and mutual problem solving.

How Do I Make Fight Right Work for Me?

Use this survey as a tool to improve your problem solving with the person you had in mind as you completed it. There are a number of ways to do this. These strategies work best at a time when the two of you are not engaged in an active disagreement.

- Show the person the scores you gave yourself on the survey, and discuss them.
- Ask the person to take the survey, and the two of you discuss your respective scores.
- Each of you uses the survey to score the conflict-resolution behavior you see in the other. Discuss why you see each other in such ways.
- Do any of the above except that both of you choose the three items you see least in the other and the three items you see most in the other. (This method is fully described in *Lemons and Oranges.*)
- Don't rate the survey items at all. Simply discuss them with each other, focusing on those that offer the greatest hope for improved problem solving between you.

Whiner Cup

Resources needed:

Winner-Whiner Chart
Whiner Cup

Tools to consult:

None

What Problems Does Whiner Cup Solve?

- Employees need to reduce their gloominess, griping, and grousing.
- I'm turning into a pessimist.

What Is the Aim of This Tool?

By now you've heard a number of "You-are-what-you . . . " claims: You are what you *wear*. You are what you *eat*. You are what you *think*. The list goes on and includes one you may not have heard: You are what you *speak*.

What does this mean? That your speech makes an indelible impression on others? Of course. But far more. "You are what you speak" means that who you are is very much determined by the words that have tripped from your lips over the years. In other words, your temperament, your present outlook, and even your success have resulted from an accumulation of your language since the day you first began to speak. Winners don't start speaking like winners after they succeed. That they speak like winners is a major reason *for* their success.

This tool reveals winner language and contrasts it with whiner language. It enables you and your team members to hold yourselves accountable for speech that will empower you to get the most out of yourselves and out of each other.

Winner-Whiner Chart

While *Whiners* Say . . .	*Winners* Say . . .
I guess.	Yes!
That looks okay.	That looks terrific.
No problem.	My pleasure.
This isn't a half-bad day.	What a beautiful day this is!
I'll try to . . .	I will . . .
I've never done it that way before.	I can't wait to do it that way.
My boss prevents me from . . .	I'll figure out a way to . . .
You make me angry.	I make myself angry.
I don't mind helping you.	*Sure* I'll help you.
We tried that before.	Let's give that another chance.
It can't be done—it won't work.	It'll be a challenge—let's go after it.
I shouldn't have . . .	It would've been better had I not . . .
I *have* to . . .	I plan to . . .
I'm not appreciated.	It's fun to do a great job.
How can you say that about me?	What causes you to say that?
When do *my* needs get met?	How can I be a better ________ to you?
You *never* . . .	I'd like to ask you to . . .
I don't know how to . . .	Up to now I've not been able to . . .
I'm too stupid, weak, fat, short, afraid to . . .	When I put my mind to it, I amaze myself.
People have to accept the way I am.	I've got some troubling habits to change.
I hope I don't blow this!	Watch me make this work!
Boy, did I just blow it!	I just learned one more way not to . . .
I'm not appreciated around here.	It's fun to do a great job!
No one tells you anything around here.	I need to figure out how to stay informed.
We're understaffed.	The amount of work we do is amazing.
Let somebody else deal with it.	Here's my chance to contribute.
Isn't it five o'clock yet?	You mean it's quitting time already?

How Does Whiner Cup Work?

Step 1: Post "Winner-Whiner Charts" in your office.

Communicate your expectations for positive language by plastering charts like the one above all around your office.

Step 2: Produce a Whiner Cup.

Write "Whiner Cup" on the side of a drinking cup. Keep it out in full view of employees. If you really take this tool seriously and you have large numbers of employees, you might contract with a specialty advertising company to mass-produce the cups.

Step 3: Establish contribution guidelines.

How much money will you and team members put in the cup whenever anyone is caught by another team member in the act of using "whiner" language? To what charity will you donate the receipts?

Step 4: Do it!

How Do I Make Whiner Cup Work for Me?

Here are a number of steps you can take toward more positive communication, in addition to establishing an office Whiner Cup.

1. Personal change. On your Winner-Whiner Chart check off the examples of whiner language that characterize your speech. In the "Personal Change Chart" below write as many as five winner statements you will use instead.

Personal Change Chart

My Typical Whiner Statements	To Be Replaced Immediately by . . .
1. ______________________	1. ______________________
2. ______________________	2. ______________________
3. ______________________	3. ______________________
4. ______________________	4. ______________________
5. ______________________	5. ______________________

2. **Feedback to and from employees.** Use the "Winner-Whiner Chart" to give feedback to employees on their language or to receive such feedback from others, employees included. One way to accomplish this that doesn't elicit defensiveness would be for the feedback giver to circle no more than five expressions on the left side and no more than five expressions on the right that he or she hears most often. Your subsequent discussion could focus on the impact on the relationship of the ten circled statements.

3. **Communication curriculum.** Introduce the "Winner-Whiner Chart" into employee training programs, particularly for those employees who interact with customers, such as front-line service providers and salespeople.

4. **Team meetings.** Take the chart and a Whiner Cup to your next team meeting to keep the meeting positive and prolific.

5 TOOLS FOR MOTIVATION

Hero Table

Resources needed:

None

Tools to consult:

Team Builder
Fight Right
Criticism Template

What Problems Does Hero Table Solve?

- I'm a praise miser.
- Employees don't feel enough ownership for the goals or the strategy of this enterprise.
- Employees need to reduce their gloominess, griping, and grousing.

What Is the Aim of This Tool?

The psychologist William James said, "The deepest principle of human nature is the craving to be appreciated." In a recent Lou Harris poll, Americans were asked what most influences their personal happiness; 28 percent volunteered the answer "positive feedback at work"—an especially impressive statistic when you consider that only about 67 percent of adult Americans are employed. Throughout the years, survey after survey of workers has consistently found that the recognition they get from their bosses has more to do with their job satisfaction than any tangible rewards they receive, including money.

As important as praise is, it appears to be in extremely short supply in the workplace. One question we like to pose to the thousands of employees we encounter in our speaking tours is "How many of you feel that you receive an appropriate amount of praise, recognition, and statements of personal appreciation from your boss for the work you do?" Over the years on average only 10 percent have felt moved to raise their hands.

This tool is for the manager who suspects that he or she might be a praise miser. It helps you to spot the praiseworthy opportunities employees present to you, and it shows you how to respond to them in a way that increases the commitment they feel to doing a good job.

How Does Hero Table Work?

There are many things an employee might do to earn your appreciation and praise. The easiest way to make sure you take advantage of the opportunities presented to you is to create a "Hero Table" like the one on page 98. Here's how to use it.

Step 1: Put the names of your team members at the top of the table.

Duplicate the table as needed to accommodate more praise recipients.

Step 2: Think of praiseworthy events.

Can you think of any to add to the list?

Step 3: Check off the praiseworthy events you expect to witness.

Over the next few weeks what victories do you anticipate? Which ones will each team member in the table most likely cause or contribute to? Place as many checks as apply in each team member column. To the right of each check write a brief description of exactly what you expect that team member to do that will earn recognition.

Step 4: Prepare to motivate your people through praise.

Study your "Hero Table" entries. If you do this each night just before you go to bed, you'll have the best chance of embedding them in your brain. During the day you can hide behind trees in ambush to surprise people with the recognition they'll appreciate.

How Do I Make Hero Table Work for Me?

Three additional analyses will be helpful before you use your Hero Table. First, you want to understand why you may be a praise miser right now. Second, you want to make sure you meet certain preconditions of effective praising. Third, you want to be sure to deliver praise in an effective manner.

Hero Table

Praiseworthy Events	✓	Team Member #1: ______ Anticipated Behavior	✓	Team Member #2: ______ Anticipated Behavior
Exceptional customer service		______ ______		______ ______
Task done efficiently or effectively		______ ______		______ ______
Problem solving		______ ______		______ ______
Saving money		______ ______		______ ______
Generating new business		______ ______		______ ______
Engaging in teamwork		______ ______		______ ______
Showing creativity or initiative		______ ______		______ ______
Accomplishing a challenging feat		______ ______		______ ______
Going beyond the call of duty		______ ______		______ ______
Helping you out		______ ______		______ ______
Making the company look good		______ ______		______ ______

1. What are your excuses for not praising enough?

Here are several reasons why supervisors often don't give the praise they should. Check off one or two that sometimes turn you into a praise miser.

___I expect the best and therefore don't get very excited when I receive it.
___I'm a high achiever who has difficulty recognizing employee accomplishments not up to my personal standards.
___I believe the stick is more motivating than the carrot.
___I have difficulty reaching out to others with warm and genuine thanks.
___I'm not always there to see or to hear about the victories of employees.
___Praise giving is not a widespread norm in my company; the boss doesn't do it.
___I don't believe in recognizing employees who just do their job and not much more.
___I'm too busy; I don't have time even to think about catching people in the act of victory.
___I'm a failure preventer rather than a success ensurer. I focus on keeping my people on the straight and narrow rather than maximizing their potential. I strive to keep a smooth running operation, not to find new and better ways of doing things.

What can you do to shake yourself out of the beliefs or situations you checked?

2. What are the preconditions of effective praise?

Before you praise, as many as possible of these conditions should exist:

- Be sincere. Don't praise to earn points with the person or because you happen to be in a good mood.
- Praise performance that the receiver believes warrants your applause.
- Select a proper place to deliver the praise—in public if possible, but in private if the praise will alienate other employees or embarrass the receiver.
- Be sure that no other deserving persons are being left out.
- Don't negate the praise by saying something like "It's about time," or "Make sure you do it that way *all* the time."

- Most important, praise the deed, not the doer. You want employees to be thus pumped up by *their work* and not by you. You also don't want them to let down after the praise, which they might do if you tell them you are happy about them instead of being excited about the quality of *their work.*

3. How can I deliver praise most effectively?

Speak your praise in no more than three sentences. Don't lay it on thick.

Sentence 1: Tell the person what event, behavior, or performance you appreciate. Remember to recognize the deed and not the doer. (Example: "That was an excellent solution you presented to that unhappy customer.")

Sentence 2: State the good that has resulted from the act for the company, for the team, for customers, or for you. (Example: "As a result, I think you just won us a customer for life.")

Sentence 3: Express how good you feel about the deed. Don't pile it on to the point of becoming sickeningly sweet. Don't make comparisons to other employees. (Example: "It's great to see such dedication on our staff," or simply "Thank you.")

Say no more: Allow your words to sink in. Leave without being abrupt.

Appraise for Success

Resources needed:

None

Tools to consult:

Culture Print
Great Expectations
Performance Pay

What Problems Does Appraise for Success Solve?

- Our performance reviews don't work; managers hate giving them, and employees hate receiving them.
- I want to tie pay to performance in such a way that people are motivated to improve their performance and enhance the bottom line.
- My employees need performance feedback that gives them priorities for professional development rather than mere judgments of their capabilities.

What Is the Aim of This Tool?

Appraise for Success will bring you employee development riches you never thought possible through the performance review process. It sets aside the typical dysfunctional employee evaluation system for one that will encourage your employees to excel.

There are two reasons for creating a formal mechanism to assess employee performance. One is to document and to justify the salary, promotion, and even disciplinary decisions you need to make about your employees. The other is to improve performance. In truth, most companies rely on performance reviews mostly for the first reason—documentation and justification. That explains why performance

Conventional Performance Review Item

Ratings (check one)

Performance factor	5 Significantly Exceeds Expectations	4 Exceeds Expectations	3 Meets Expectations	2 Falls Below Expectations	1 Falls Significantly Below Expectations
Communication skills					

Comments: ______________________________

review forms in their systems bear a strong resemblance to the example shown above.

Formats like that one ask the supervisor to rate several factors of employee performance on a scale with as few as three levels or as many as ten levels, with five levels the norm. Sometimes descriptions of the five levels of achievement are substituted for a numerical scale; often both a numerical and a descriptive scale are included. Raters are encouraged to provide additional comments. The factors rated vary from company to company and often from job level to job level within the same company. Some commonly rated performance factors are communication skills, initiative, responsibility, punctuality, creativity, reliability, teamwork, quality, productivity, customer focus, and leadership.

Occasionally employees are asked to do a self-evaluation. The idea is to get employees thinking about their performance prior to the performance review meeting and to encourage a dialogue rather than a monologue.

Such systems are highly favored by many managers and especially human-resources professionals because they quantify performance in a way that helps them to justify their personnel decisions. You can sum scores, or average them, and link these outcomes to a merit pay system—say, that employees who get 3.75 or above are eligible for more than a cost-of-living increase.

If you have personal experience with this type of performance review, you're probably not too happy with it—your stomach probably gets tied in knots just before each face-to-face meeting. Further, employees being rated rarely receive value from the appraisal. Why these problems? Because the traditional performance review system has these flaws.

1. Usually some of the performance factors included on rating forms bear little resemblance to what is truly important in the job of the person being rated.
2. Any scale, whether consisting of numbers or descriptions of achievement, is little more than a labeling system. Raters aren't comfortable labeling people, and people don't want to be labeled.
3. No two people interpret a rating scale the same way. Therefore, one rater's 3.75 may equal a more lenient rater's 4.25.
4. A system that focuses heavily on quantitative results, such as a total score or average of scores received on performance factors, encourages employees to focus on those scores rather than on the corrective actions they need to take to improve their performance. ("I'm satisfied—I got my 4.0.")
5. On a five-point scale, raters rarely circle either the 1 ("Why is that person still working here?") or the 5 ("That employee walks on water."). The result in many companies is, for all practical purposes, a three-point scale.
6. The descriptions of achievement are often inconsistent with the interpretation of the numbers. For instance, most employees would be unhappy to receive a 3 out of 5 on a performance factor. Yet the description corresponding to a 3 is typically "commendable" or "meets expectations." Should employees be upset to have their work termed "commendable"? If "meets expectations" is not a good rating, does that say our expectations are too low?
7. The comments section is rarely used for meaningful commentary. A rater who gives an employee a score of 4 out of 5 on communication skills is likely to add beneath the score that "the employee is an effective communicator." Of what possible value is such a statement?

Employees, managers, and their companies deserve better. This tool gives it to them in a performance review system that deemphasizes numerical ratings and calculations, focuses on performance factors that really mean something, provides feedback that gets noticed and taken seriously, and holds the rater fully accountable for the judgments given.

How Does Appraise for Success Work?

Step 1: Generate expectations.

This tool supports an expectation-based performance review. Create those expectations with the help of *Great Expectations.* If you implement *Culture Print*, the expectations will come from that document.

Step 2: Create your performance review form.

A page from a sample Appraise for Success form shown below is based on the core value of Teamwork generated in *Culture Print.* Your final performance review form may contain a similar page of feedback for each of the core values you choose to assess.

Sample Page from Appraise for Success Form

Core value area: Teamwork

1. Share information and knowledge with others.
   - Impart needed information to coworkers and supervisors.
   - Share new ideas and recommend process improvements.
   - Express clearly your needs and expectations to related departments.
   - Keep supervisors informed of your problems and your achievements.
   - Share lessons learned from failures and successes.
   - Advise your supervisor when you see opportunities for better use of the team.
2. Support others.
   - Obtain a thorough understanding of situations with other employees before you form an opinion.
   - Work through proper channels to bring about change.
   - Cooperate with the direction provided by your supervisor.
   - Strive to make "downstream" operations a success.
   - Provide exceptional internal customer service.
   - Be a positive role model to those around you.
   - Help and encourage employees in all departments and divisions.

3. Respect others.

   - Don't interrupt others or create distractions.
   - Treat others as equals; be considerate of them.
   - Don't gossip.
   - Don't be a chronic complainer.
   - Don't criticize others behind their backs.
   - Resolve disagreements directly and professionally.
   - Arrive on time for meetings.

How well are the expectations within this value area currently being fulfilled?

___ Completely (100 percent)
___ Significantly (90–99 percent)
___ Mostly (80–89 percent)
___ Partially (70–79 percent)
___ Poorly (0–69 percent)

Of the seven core values, what is the relative priority of this one (first through seventh)?

____

What does the employee need to do more or less of to evidence complete fulfillment of the expectations within this value area? (Describe specific behaviors to be manifested and measurable goals to be achieved.)

____
____
____

What is the employee doing very well in this area, and should continue doing?

____
____
____

What training, coaching, or other form of professional development should the employee receive?

____
____
____

Step 3: Use your Appraise for Success form.

Train managers how to use Appraise for Success properly. Like any performance review methodology, this tool requires time and care. Managers will do themselves and employees a disservice by filling out the form on the run or squeezing it between two other "more important" tasks. The first time around, have them plan to spend at least 15 minutes with each value area, and set aside at least 45 minutes for the actual performance review meetings. One of the beauties of this tool is that subsequent ratings and interviews will take less time as they become increasingly effective.

When you provide feedback on what employees need to do to fulfill expectations completely, that feedback must be related to one or more of the expectations already included in the area being assessed. If you are tempted to point to extraneous factors not covered by an expectation, add new expectations to cover those factors.

Consider having employees perform a self-evaluation prior to their meeting with supervisors. If you think this is too much, ask them to rank how well they believe they fulfill the expectations in each core-value area. Discussing their rankings will prove to be to valuable icebreaker at the performance review meeting.

Most companies withhold the performance review form from the sight of employees until it is filled out for the first time as a judgment of their behavior. What a horrible mistake! Show it to job candidates at the employment interview. Use it as a basis for new-employee orientation. Have it handy whenever you coach or mentor employees.

The more often you conduct the performance review, the more it will reinforce employee accountability. Once a year is the minimum frequency that you can expect to have a significant impact on employee performance. Once every six months is better. Once every four months is better yet. Once every three months is ideal.

How Do I Make Appraise for Success Work for Me?

Yes, this format requires more action from supervisors than checking boxes on a form. But consider all the advantages of the Appraise for Success format:

1. Raters evaluate performance based on the requirements of the job.

2. The quantitative feedback that employees receive (e.g., the percentage check-off) is determined by their fulfillment of performance expectations, not by an abitary rating system.
3. If raters cannot check the "Completely (100 percent)" category, they must tell employees exactly what the latter must do to attain that level of achievement on a subsequent review.
4. Employees learn the relative importance of correcting each area in which they receive feedback by seeing the relative priority supervisors place on each value area.
5. Employees receive specific written suggestions for improving their performance.
6. Employees receive written affirmation of their most commendable actions.
7. Employees receive guidance on specific development actions they can take to improve their performance.

Salary 101

Resources needed:

Income Chart
Flip chart
Markers

Tools to consult:

Performance Pay

What Problems Does Salary 101 Solve?

- Employees claim, "We don't get paid our fair share, given all the money this company makes."
- Employees don't feel enough ownership for the goals or the strategy of this enterprise.
- How can I make our employees more cost-conscious?

What Is the Aim of This Tool?

We all view the world through perceptual filters. One of those filters is created by either signing a paycheck (buying labor) or cashing the check (selling labor). Many employees, because they are on the selling end of the transaction, have incorrect (usually inflated) perceptions about their relative worth in the labor market. This is especially true for employees who have neither offered their services to a competitor nor purchased fringe benefits, such as health insurance, independent of the company plan.

Many employees have incorrect or distorted views concerning sales, profits, and cash flow. For example, some believe that whenever inventory is moving out the door or clients are being served the company *must* be making money. Your employees have all heard that "it takes money to make money," but they may not fully understand what that means.

Salary 101 provides employees with a few basic lessons in economics and accounting. This tool reveals financial information about the company. As a result, employees learn that sales don't necessarily equal profits and an employee's worth is a function of the value he or she provides. Once employees learn these lessons, they develop a greater appreciation for their total compensation and may even develop a vested interest in cutting costs.

The knee-jerk reaction of many owners and managers to this idea is that the company's books should be open only to their accountant, their banker, and the IRS. They believe that the only financial information employees need is the size of their paycheck. These are often the same managers who have trouble getting employees to search for cost-saving or money-making opportunities. These are often the same managers who see a net brain drain away from their company and to their competition. These are the same managers who are losing out to those who have discovered that opening the books, sharing the profits, and revealing cash flow is a win-win proposition.

How Does Salary 101 Work?

Salary 101 is based on a philosophy of "open-book management." It's based on an "Income Chart" that is filled out by employees and discussed at a three-hour training program.

Step 1: Ask participants to complete the "Income Chart."

Ask participants to answer the questions in the "Income Chart" (on page 110) on the basis of their current knowledge or beliefs. If they aren't sure about an answer, they should guess, rounding off answers to the nearest $1,000. Tell them not to worry about getting the right answers—they will not be graded or evaluated in any way.

Step 2: Conduct a three-hour training program using the chart as a starting point.

Part 1: Reveal the correct answers to the questions. Answer any questions about the financial terms used on the chart. Lead a discussion of the meaning of the correct answers and what they say about the state of the company.

Part 2: Draw attention to lines 4 and 5. Many employees will be surprised at the size of the payroll and thus at how costly even a modest across-the-board pay increase is. Even more are likely to be surprised by the expense of their fringe-benefits package. Be prepared to be thrown some tough questions here; for instance,

Income Chart

Question	Your Answer	Correct Answer
1. How much was our total revenue (or sales) last year?	______	______
2. How much other income did we earn from sources such as interest, securities, or royalties?	______	______
3. Add lines 1 and 2 to get our total income.	______	______
4. How much did we pay out in direct salary, wages, and bonuses?	______	______
5. How much in addition did we pay out in the form of fringe benefits, pensions, and severance to our employees?	______	______
6. How much were our other operating expenses such as materials, supplies, postage, advertising, printing, travel, and the like?	______	______
7. What charges did we have for the depreciation of equipment and our facilities?	______	______
8. What were our overhead (or fixed) costs such as insurance, utilities, maintenance, and rent?	______	______
9. What were our interest expenses on loans we needed to take out?	______	______
10. Add up lines 4–9 to get our total expenses.	______	______
11. Subtract line 10 from line 3 to get before-tax profit.	______	______
12. How much tax (federal, state, local) did we pay last year?	______	______
13. Subtract line 12 from line 11 to get net profit.	______	______
14. How much of net profit was paid out to the owners (or shareholders) of the business?	______	______
15. How much of net profit was reinvested in our business to grow or to increase our ability to compete effectively?	______	______

the relative amounts paid out to salaried managers versus hourly wage-earning employees.

Part 3: Focus on the costs in lines 6–10 and 11. Many employees take these for granted. Be prepared to explain depreciation.

Part 4: Finally, help employees understand that in any business the people who have risked their money to fund the company—its owners—have the first call on profits. After that, the company must reinvest in itself to remain competitive. The bottom line is for employees to realize that even in time of high profits, there's not a lot of free money floating around, and they aren't the only ones who have invested themselves to generate it.

How Do I Make Salary 101 Work for Me?

Don't use this tool if your numbers are embarrassing.

Use common sense. Some companies should be glad their employees don't have access to the books. However, if your management and ownership are behaving responsibly and fairly, you have everything to gain and nothing to lose.

Conduct Salary 101 in conjunction with Performance Pay.

Employees who don't trust management and who don't know the financial numbers may assume that your gain-sharing plan is shortchanging them.

Prepare to share and discuss financial information.

In order to achieve the goals of Steps 1 and 2 you must be prepared to share any financial information that is known by your auditors. Be prepared to answer the toughest of questions with the greatest of candor. Anything less than full disclosure will almost certainly backfire. Even so, you may need to announce at the beginning that not all questions can be answered. For example, no personal financial information will be revealed.

Provide comparative data on compensation and other costs.

This question is bound to arise: "How do we compare in compensation [or other] costs with . . . ?" Even before it does, answer it. Show employees where you stand on the Income Chart in relation to the competition. That you *offer* to do this is further evidence of your desire to be candid.

Train as if you were conducting a life-saving class, not an accounting class.

For the training to have maximum impact, it should be lively, engaging, and practical. Bring in actual sales orders and discuss the costs required to produce those sales. Bring in canceled orders and discuss the loss (sunk and actual) because a dissatisfied customer took business elsewhere. Discuss the implications of lost sales on total compensation and business expansion.

Is there someone on your payroll who can talk financial data and keep you on the edge of your seat? That's the person who should conduct the training.

You want each employee to walk out of the training sessions with the same conclusion: The only job security I have is making sure I provide value for the dollar paid me for my labor.

Reveal the data on an ongoing basis that you want employees to track.

If you want employees to focus on data and trends, put that information in newsletters, on posters, and on inserts in their pay envelopes. How many units were sold this week? How does that compare to the same week last year? How did the average cost per unit of sales this week compare with the same week a year ago? Are operating costs increasing or decreasing? What items in operating costs warrant close scrutiny? Is market share increasing or decreasing? How do our production and sales figures compare with industrial averages? If you want employees to talk to one another about savings, increasing sales, reducing waste, and increasing productivity, immerse them in a culture where these concepts are pervasive.

Incorporate Salary 101 into new-employee orientation.

Set the stage for what you want employees to know about the financial reality of running the business. Drive home the principle that salaries are paid by satisfied customers—not managers, not stockholders, and not boards of directors. Get them so attuned to the monetary issues of your operation that there will be no need for them ever to attend a Salary 101 session.

Resources needed:

None

Tools to consult:

Culture Print
Appraise for Success
Salary 101
Team Links

Performance Pay

What Problems Does Performance Pay Solve?

- Employees don't feel enough ownership of the goals or the strategy of this enterprise.
- I want to tie pay to performance in such a way that people are motivated to improve their performance and enhance the bottom line.

What Is the Aim of This Tool?

We've learned our lesson. Automatic pay increases based on seniority are bad news, for both employers and employees. They hurt employers by removing a vital incentive from the motivational arsenal and by increasing the payroll as the workforce ages, even though that workforce may not collectively be making productivity gains. They hurt employees whose bloated salaries target them as attractive sources of cost cutting and when deadweights receive the same rewards as dedicated workers.

On the other hand, relatively few companies that have embarked on merit pay plans are fully pleased with the results. No wonder. The flaws in many of these procedures are legion.

The worst among them reveal the weaknesses below. Check off those that are valid criticisms of a system you are familiar with.

___ The specific criteria for increases are not shared with employees.
___ The criteria for increases include performance review procedures that employees do not respect.
___ The criteria for increases include performance measures that employees do not believe are a valid yardstick of their accomplishments.
___ The criteria for increases include performance measures that are highly subjective and rely on the arbitrary judgment of supervisors.
___ The criteria for increases include performance measures that encourage employees to maximize short-term results at the expense of long-term outcomes.
___ The merit increases are so small in relation to existing pay levels that employees are not encouraged to strive for them.
___ Employees so mistrust management that they are convinced that pay decisions are based on favoritism rather than merit.
___ The performance measures used are not under the control of employees; they don't have complete ability to affect them.
___ Increases reward individual accomplishments, and not the teams that support those accomplishments, thereby discouraging teamwork.
___ The system has been shoved down the throats of employees who for whatever reason do not favor differential pay based on performance measures.

Performance Pay will help you create a compensation formula that steers you around most of these problems. You'll emerge with a pay plan that encourages your employees to cut costs, increase income, and turn your company into a perennial winner.

How Does Performance Pay Work?

This tool is linked to two other tools in this book, *Appraise for Success* and *Salary 101.* The relationship is a simple one. The more fully employees meet the requirements you establish for their performance and the more they help you to reduce operating costs, the more they should be financially rewarded. But exactly how can you forge a link between performance and pay while avoiding the problems described in the previous section?

Step 1: Distinguish between raises and gain-sharing.

Raises accumulate, thereby increasing the base of employee compensation each year; *gain-sharing* is granted on a one-time basis and does not elevate base pay. Generally speaking, gain-sharing (bonuses, profit sharing) is preferable to raises, which continue to reward employees for years after the effort that earned them and often have the ultimate impact of pricing consistently good employees out of the market.

Raises are best used to reward employees for permanent improvements they make in their personal value to the company though training or other forms of professional development. When you choose to give raises, establish in advance the personal improvement criteria that employees understand will lead to specific dollar or percentage increases.

Gain-sharing is best used to reward employees for improvements they have caused in operations or other bottom-line measures. Gain-sharing funds can be drawn from year-end profits in response to outstanding performance, or they can be drawn from one-time cost savings or revenue enhancements resulting from employee initiatives.

Step 2: Allocate funds for gain-sharing.

Decide what dollar amount of profits will be allocated to the gain-sharing pool. Next create a scheme that enables employees to earn "shares" though their performance. That scheme might be linked to an expectation-based performance appraisal procedure as shown on the next page.

When your choice is cost-saving or revenue-enhancement gain-sharing, determine in advance what cost-saving or revenue-enhancing results will qualify and what percentage of those savings or increases will be awarded to responsible employees. See page 117 for advice on how to use this type of gain-sharing.

Gain-sharing plans typically kick in only after a certain level of profit—sufficient to pay back investors or owners—has been achieved.

Step 3: Tie gain-sharing to team performance.

Gain-sharing will have a positive impact on teamwork when it is tied not only to individual proficiency but also to team accomplishment. Gain-sharing should also be tied to the quality of internal customer service that departments provide to each other. (See *Team Links.*)

***Step 4: Run* Salary 101.**

Show employees how their performance affects the bottom line. Tell them the basics of your gain-sharing program.

How Do I Make Performance Pay Work for Me?

In this section are two examples of gain-sharing. The first is based on net profits, the second on cost savings. Neither is presented as a model to follow, but rather as an example. You may choose to use one of these plans as a guideline with numbers appropriate to your company and to your industry plugged in. Or you may choose to create your own plan from scratch. Either way, you might want to appoint a committee of employees to recommend a plan that they believe will work best.

Example #1: A year-end performance gain-sharing plan

To fully understand this "Year-End Performance-Based Gain-Sharing Plan," consult *Appraise for Success.* The plan is based on the sample performance review form provided in that tool. It covers hourly employees, and you may choose to distribute a separate amount to salaried employees.

Year-End Performance-Based Gain-sharing Plan

Gain-sharing Allocation

Reserve 50% of net profits that are over and above a 12% return on equity for the hourly-wage employees covered by this plan.

Criteria for earning shares

1. In the three top-priority value areas on the *Appraise for Success* performance review form, employees earn these shares for fulfillment-of-expectations levels on the most recent review:
   - 5 shares for "Completely"
   - 4 shares for "Significantly"
   - 3 shares for "Mostly"
   - 2 shares for "Partially"

2. In the remaining value areas on the *Appraise for Success* performance review, employees earn these shares for checked fulfillment-of-expectations levels on the most recent review:
   - 4 shares for "Completely"
   - 3 shares for "Significantly"
   - 2 shares for "Mostly"
   - 1 share for "Partially"
3. Additional shares are awarded for these accomplishments:
   - 3 shares for perfect attendance
   - 2 shares for taking only one or two sick days in the calendar year
   - 1 share for taking three or four sick days in the calendar year
   - 1 share for each half day spent in training
   - 2 shares for serving on any approved employee task forces, committees, or focus groups
   - 5 shares for membership on the "Team of the Month"
   - 4 shares for winning "Employee of the Month"
   - 4 shares for winning performance awards (see *Players On the Bench*)
   - 5 shares for working in the "Department of the Year" (see *Team Links*)
   - 2 shares for each submitted idea accepted for implementation by the Quality Improvement Committee; 3 additional shares for ideas named as "Idea of the Month"; 10 additional shares for the employee suggestion named as "Idea of the Year"

Performance pay calculation

Sum the total number of shares earned by all employees covered under this plan. Divide them into the total gain-sharing funds available to get the value of each share. Example: The 100 employees of a company with a profit exceeding a 12% return on investment by $400,000 have generated among themselves 3,300 shares throughout the year, making the value of one share $61 (50 percent of $400,000 divided by 3,300). An employee who earned 33 shares under the criteria listed in the example would receive an end-of-year gain-share of $2,000.

Example #2: A cost-savings gain-sharing plan

The purpose of this plan is to encourage employees to look for ways to save money for the company. A portion of the documented savings they achieve is shared with them as a reward for their efforts and as an incentive to continue their search for cost reductions.

Cost-Savings–Based Gain-sharing Plan

Gain-sharing allocation

For documented cost savings, employees receive:

- 10% of the gain for savings up to $10,000
- 9% for $10,001–$25,000
- 8% for $25,001–$50,000
- 7% for $50,001–$100,000
- 6% for $100,001–$200,000
- 5% for $200,001–$500,000
- 4% for $500,001–$1,000,000
- 3% for savings over $1,000,000

To reinforce the role that teams play in cost savings, 50 percent of the dollar amount otherwise due to the individual(s) whose idea created the savings will be distributed among the members of the work team who directly or indirectly supported the recognized individual.

Criteria for allocation

All claims for cost savings are submitted to the cost-savings/gain-sharing committee for verification that the cost reduction resulted from an extraordinary effort and was not merely an expected outcome from the individual's, or the team's, everyday duties. The committee also verifies the actual amount of cost savings to be credited to the employee and identifies the team members who will receive a portion of the gain-sharing.

The chief administrator responsible for the cost-savings program is charged with ensuring that the program avoids an inordinate fixation on cost reduction—particularly at the expense of revenue generation—and does not encourage the inflation of supposed cost savings on the basis of hypothetical expenses, which were never actually incurred in the past.

Cash, stock, or retirement fund?

Some companies dispense gain-sharing in the form of cash, others prefer to award stock in the company, and still others make a contribution in kind to the employees' retirement fund. In making your choice, keep two considerations in mind. One is the advice of your accountant. The other is which of these forms of payment will have the desired impact of spurring employees on to greater quality and quantity of effort.

Home Links

Resources needed:

Varies, depending on the strategies selected

Tools to consult:

Balance
Envision

What Problems Does Home Links Solve?

- We need to make sure the families of our employees don't feel neglected and abused because of the workload imposed on their family members.
- We want our employees to get maximum support from home.

What Is the Aim of This Tool?

If you had asked a group of employees in the 1950s what the most important reason was for them to work, you might have heard something like "to put food on the table." Ask a group of employees today that same question, and you're more likely to hear "to put food on the table *and* to share that meal with my family." Balance might have been a strange idea for our parents; it is a defining value for us and our children. Today's employee will not commit to employers who expect family and health to be sacrificed for the sake of market share or return on equity.

Unfortunately, the need for personal balance coexists uneasily with organizations' increasing need to be better, smarter, leaner, and quicker than the competition. Given this pressure to perform, we should not be surprised that many employees feel they are unhappily stretched to the limits of their physical and emotional endurance. The result leaves little time for life outside work.

But there is good news. More and more companies today are finding ways to become "family friendly," thereby reducing the tension between life and work—as well they should. Companies that successfully attract and retain talent are those that help employees create a personal balance. That balance is reflected in increased energy and commitment, which ultimately result in higher profits. How do companies create that balance and reap the rewards? They create bridges or links with the family.

How Does Home Links Work?

Home Links is a collection of related programs and policies. In total, they are designed to help employees balance the pressure and demands of the job with their commitments to their families. The rationale of these ideas is that families who are committed to the company will find ways to help the employee manage and negotiate the demands of the job and will have more tolerance for the sacrifices they are asked to make. Which of these ideas will work best for you?

1. A welcome letter to a new hire's family.

Welcome the entire family to the company. Tell them how happy and proud you are to have the new employee and the family as part of your extended corporate family. In the letter describe all the family services they are now eligible for. Follow the letter up with a fruit basket delivered to the home.

2. Kindnesses to the family of a hospitalized or convalescing employee.

Visit hospitalized or convalescing employees. Send flowers. Call or visit the family. Let them know that you are available to provide whatever help you can. Assure them that their loved one is missed and will be welcomed back with open arms when he or she is fully recovered.

3. Recognize family milestones and achievements.

Acknowledge birthdays and wedding anniversaries. Send congratulatory notes to employees' children who graduate or achieve other honors in their communities.

4. Give employee discounts on company products or services.

Seek profits from customers, not employees. Provide goods and services at cost. Your employees and their families will appreciate the largesse and are likely to respond with greater loyalty. You might also share corporate discounts on home computers or raffle off outdated corporate computers.

5. Employee discounts from suppliers.

When you negotiate with suppliers, factor in discounts for your employees on suppliers' goods and services.

6. Give bonuses and gifts with a distinctly family flavor.

When running contests or in-house competitions, give prizes that reward families as well as individuals. For example:

- An escape weekend
- Providing a videographer to record the family's next life-cycle celebration
- Providing the labor, materials, or both for remodeling an employee's kitchen or bathroom
- Free maid service for a month
- Dinner out or a catered holiday meal

7. Award scholarships.

One of our clients awards postsecondary school scholarships to the most needy and meritorious high school students of employees who earn less than a stipulated amount.

8. Offer access to equipment and supplies for family members' projects.

A tool and die shop lets employees and family members use machines for personal projects on the weekends. An auto repair shop provides space and equipment where employees and their families can work on their own cars.

9. Subsidize employee philanthropy.

Have you ever noticed the company spirit and family support during company-sponsored food drives and toy drives? Whenever a company helps their employees feed the hungry at Thanksgiving or put toys in children's hands at Christmas, everyone associated with the company gets a warm glow.

Some companies give employees one day off with pay to donate to community projects such as Habitat for Humanity.

10. Create a company-sponsored Employee Assistance Program (EAP).

Whenever one of your employees has a personal problem or feels inundated by the demands and pressures of the job, he should be able to get confidential professional guidance and counseling. You might also provide access to marriage and family counseling. Contact a local mental health agency or hospital in your town to find out how to set up a program.

How Do I Make Home Links Work for Me?

Build Home Links goals into your yearly planning and budgeting.

Wishing will not make it so. Budgeting and tracking will. Commitment to bridging work and home is ultimately measured by the resources a company devotes to that bridge.

Establish a family-friendly task force.

A standing committee signifies the importance of an issue. If you want to walk the talk of personal balance, support a standing committee or task force to provide analysis and advice. The task force should focus on policies and strategies that help employees balance the pressures of work with the commitments at home. You might also ask a few family members to sit on the committee.

Establish policies, procedures, and bonuses that support families but are nondiscriminatory.

Enable employees who don't have a traditional family at home to reap the benefits of Home Links.

Brown Bag

Resources needed:

Assigned reading or seminar material

Tools to consult:

Vista

What Problems Does Brown Bag Solve?

- My employees aren't taking responsibility for their personal development.
- We need to know the latest in management development but don't have the time for off-site training.
- How can we get greater impact from the training we do?

What Is the Aim of This Tool?

Just as every new generation of computer comes out with a more powerful microprocessor, so too must every successful company expand its ability to acquire and assimilate new information. In the vernacular of organization theorists, successful companies are "learning organizations" that increase the intellectual capital represented by their employees. Brown Bag will help you and your team achieve this goal and thereby increase your ability to compete.

If there is one truism about the new millennium, it is that successful companies will be those with an insatiable hunger for new information. They will ensure that all employees have state-of-the-art knowledge and are constantly learning. They will recognize the undisputed value of "intellectual capital" and constantly add to it. Unsuccessful companies will stop learning. Their appetite for information is already satisfied; they see no need to empower employees with state-of-the-art knowledge. For these companies the phrase "intellectual capital" is little more than management jargon.

Brown Bag increases your employees' knowledge base at minimum cost. Rather than bringing in high-priced management gurus or taking time out of your schedule to attend seminars and courses, you incorporate continuous learning inexpensively and efficiently into your operation. When you implement this tool, everyone in the company will embrace continuous learning as a personal responsibility, and that value will weave itself into the corporate culture.

How Does Brown Bag Work?

Brown Bag consists of inexpensive, educational sessions conducted during breakfast or lunch. You and your employees schedule time together to discuss a book, listen to a presentation, watch a video, or discuss an important issue facing the company. The seminars are designed by you and your team, conducted by you and your team, and will help everyone on the team learn and grow. To bring this tool into your company follow these guidelines.

1. Schedule them on a regular basis.

One of our clients schedules a 90-minute "power breakfast" the last Friday of every month. Because the meeting is part of the office calendar, employees view the meeting as integral to the corporate culture. When a holiday falls on a Friday, the meeting is moved to a different day of the week.

2. Provide either the full meal or a portion of it.

Some companies ask employees to provide their own food, but provide at least the beverage or dessert, in the case of lunch. Other companies provide the full meal. Employees should not feel that they are "giving up" their lunch hour, but rather taking advantage of an opportunity for growth and advancement. Providing the meal or part of it makes the session more palatable.

3. Maintain tight control over the agenda.

The sole purpose of this meeting is to discuss and explore cutting-edge issues related to management strategies and techniques. These are not gripe, "gotcha," or "bull" sessions. You and your employees are getting together over lunch (or breakfast) to increase your skills and abilities. Any other agenda is tangential at best and irrelevant at worst.

4. Rotate the leadership for each session.

Responsibility for leading the discussion and selecting the agenda rotates among team members. This ensures that continuous learning and self-improvement are everyone's responsibility. Leaders are not expected to be, nor should they assume, the role of content experts. They simply initiate, facilitate, and conclude the discussion.

5. Vary seminar materials.

You can use books, videotapes, audiotapes, magazine articles, presentations from major suppliers or customers, or presentations from employees with specialized expertise. Vary the content and the methodology of the sessions to achieve your dual goals of involving employees and increasing their skills.

6. If you decide to use printed material, select from the most interesting and authoritative sources.

Consider the following sources of topics:

- A book from the *Business Week* best-seller list
- The lead article of your trade or association journal
- An article from the *Harvard Business Review*
- An article from *Fortune, Forbes,* or *Business Week*
- A monthly selection from *Executive Book Summaries*
- An article from *Sloan Management Review* or *Business Horizons*
- A technical update from one of your suppliers
- A nonfiction book on the *New York Times* best-seller list
- A book or article recommended by a professor at your local college or university
- A story or editorial from the *Wall Street Journal*
- A presentation by an employee on a particular skill he or she possesses
- A series of minitopics that a local teacher, professor, or speaker might provide at low cost

One of our clients appoints a three-person task force to select the seminar materials. Another contracts with a management professor to select the materials.

7. If you use printed material, distribute a copy of the book or article to each participant at least one month before the session where it will be discussed.

The leader of the session assumes responsibility for distributing the material for that session. Everyone comes to the seminar prepared to discuss the assigned topic. Participants should be expected to meet their obligation of reading the material and being prepared to discuss the issues.

In the case of books, if the book is on audiotape, consider offering participants the choice of one or the other. Whether you use books or tapes, provide them free or at subsidized cost. One of our clients provides seminar participants with a yearly subscription to *Executive Book Summaries,* which condenses each of the latest management books into eight pages. We have other clients who believe that employees are more likely to assume ownership for personal development if they pay for part of their personal library.

8. Focus the agenda on key training outcomes.

The most important outcomes are the following:

- What lessons can we draw regarding our company?
- What lessons can you draw personally?
- What are the major implications for customer service? Profitability? Strategy? Employee relations? Quality improvement?
- What do you see as the most important "take-away" (i.e., application)?
- What is the most important lesson learned from this session to improve the bottom line of this company?

How Do I Make Brown Bag Work for Me?

Make sure top management attends and is involved.

The central message of this tool is that everyone is responsible for self-improvement. The best endorsement for these sessions is attendance by senior managers.

Choose a time that best fits in with everyone's schedule, and stick to it.

One way to walk the talk about personal development and continuous learning is to support it with a fixed corporate calendar. Once your team realizes that every third Thursday at noon is their time to learn, they will build that goal and the associated values into their thinking.

Relate the concepts from the seminars into the day-to-day activities of the business.

You're not running an adult education center; you're running a business. Unless you and your team can relate the theory and cases presented in the readings to the reality of serving customers and making a profit, you can find a better way to spend everyone's time. Approach the seminars with a pragmatic question: How will this help us today?

Be generous in your financial support of Brown Bag.

If the lunch you provide is one of participants' finest midday meals of the month, people will come. If employees see their colleagues enjoying books and tapes distributed at the sessions, people will come. If they learn that from time to time a top-level executive or management guru will be on hand to speak on a cutting-edge issue, they will come.

Aftermath

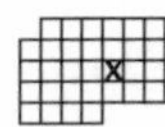

Resources needed:

Facilitator
3x5-inch index cards
Flip charts
Post-it notes
Large meeting room

Tools to consult:

Gripe Session

What Problems Does Aftermath Solve?

- We've just had a major downsizing. What can I do to start building the team again?
- Our people have a great deal of pent-up anger and hostility. How can we vent it constructively and move forward as a team?

What Is the Aim of This Tool?

Survivors of downsizing can be compared to soldiers walking off the battlefield. They may not all be physically wounded, but they are emotionally scarred. This tool is designed to help the survivors recover from the trauma as quickly as possible. Aftermath focuses on the most common wounds of downsizing: the loss of security and the severing of emotional bonds with coworkers.

The loss of psychological security creates the first emotional wound. Whether you or a coworker receives the pink slip, you now realize that your employer no longer guarantees job security, even for the best performers. And if your self-identity is inextricably linked with your job, you hope and pray that you will always have that job. You need it as much for your ego as for your checking account.

Severing bonds with coworkers creates the second wound. For many of you reading this book, a coworker is not only a team member but also your closest friend. You spend eight hours or more a day together, enjoy one another's company during lunch and breaks, share the joys and pain of your family life, and may even socialize together after work.

How Does Aftermath Work?

Aftermath heals the wounds of downsizing as quickly as possible. By means of a day-long "town meeting," employees constructively vent anger and begin building communication bridges with management. This tool is designed to achieve three goals:

1. To communicate management's recognition of and empathy with the wounds created by downsizing
2. To provide team members with an opportunity to vent their anger and frustration constructively
3. To clear up any confusion that the downsizing may have created

Because of the strong emotions created by downsizing (or any major organizational shake-up) and the need to heal as quickly as possible, you should contract with a professional group facilitator to take your group through the ten steps of the Aftermath meeting. The approximate time required for each step is in parentheses.

Step 1: Message from management (30 minutes).

Start the meeting by acknowledging the difficult time all employees have gone through and setting the stage for a bright and hopeful future. At a minimum, touch on the following themes:

- We must be as honest with one another as we possibly can so that we can begin healing today.
- We live and work in difficult times requiring difficult measures. We did what we had to do to save the company.
- We lost sleep and felt anguish as we agonized over these gut-wrenching decisions.
- Many loyal and productive employees had to be cut. We will always be grateful for their commitment to us, to their jobs, to our customers, and to you.
- Many of our friends are no longer here. We will miss them all.
- We are here to build a new future, not rehash a past.

The tone of this speech should be compassionate and upbeat. Speak from the heart, not from the overhead projector. Conclude your brief comments by introducing the facilitator. Summarize his or her credentials and reinforce the importance of having a professional assist the team to vent emotions and heal. The facilitator will lead the group through the remaining steps.

Step 2: Individual identification of anger and pain, and small-group discussion (one hour).

Issue a pad of Post-it notes to participants with the instructions to write one or more statements of the anger or pain that they now feel as a result of the downsizing. Have them post the notes on large sheets of flip-chart paper in full view. Once they do this, form them into small discussion groups of six to eight employees. Give them 30 to 45 minutes to go around the group so that participants can all explain what they wrote down.

Undoubtedly, anger and frustration will be discussed in the group, as it should be. Catharsis is a necessary step toward healing. Moreover, discussion among peers will reinforce the feeling that everyone shares the sense of loss and that everyone must pull together to move forward. There may be one or two members who will use the group as an opportunity to lambaste the company and its policies. That's okay. It needs to be said, and it needs to be heard.

Step 3: Post anger and pain statements (45 minutes).

Employees must express their anger and pain beyond their peer group, and management must hear and see it. For a large group, the front wall will be covered with Post-it notes on flip-chart sheets. The visual effect will be dramatic. The facilitator scans the notes as they are placed, looking for themes and key issues. Participants and management are also encouraged to do a "walk-by" to get the big picture of what's being said.

Step 4: Facilitator summarizes major themes expressed in the notes (30 minutes).

What are the major themes? What are the sources of the most prevalent concerns? To what extent are the firings a violation of trust, a loss of security, or something else?

Step 5: Management responds to the facilitator's summary (30 minutes).

This step acknowledges and validates employee concerns. Management must not debate or discount the facilitator's summary. Neither should leaders minimize or invalidate employee anger or pain. Quite the opposite—managers should listen nondefensively. They should empathize with the feelings of employees and thank them for their honesty. If managers discover the existence of widespread misunderstandings, they will want to clear these up, but without defending themselves.

Step 6: Small groups generate questions (45 minutes).

In their original small groups participants come up with two or three consensus questions they would like to ask management. Each question is written on a 3×5-inch card and is collected by the facilitator.

Step 7: The facilitator scans all cards looking for major clusters and themes (15 minutes).

Questions are clustered to reflect underlying themes and issues. The one or two central questions within each cluster are read out loud.

Step 8: Management answers the questions summarized by the facilitator (75 minutes).

The key to this step is honesty. Be clear, direct, and forthright.

Step 9: Facilitator summarizes the day's activities (45 minutes).

The facilitator should achieve three goals during this summary statement:

1. Highlight the important themes discussed that day.
2. Reinforce basic human-relations principles necessary for healing and growth, such as honesty, empathy, listening, validation, and communication.
3. Recommend additional actions that management and employees should pursue to continue the healing process.

Step 10: Management delivers a concluding message (30 minutes).

At a minimum, management's conclusion should cover these topics:

- Thank participants for their participation and candor.
- Emphasize the importance of healing and moving forward.
- Stress the importance of teamwork.

- Reinforce the facilitator's conclusion.
- Commit support to the facilitator's recommendations for additional actions.

How Do I Make Aftermath Work for Me?

Conduct the "town meeting" as soon as possible following the downsizing.

The longer you wait, the longer you delay the necessary healing, and the more you allow negative attitudes to become fixed.

Compose breakout groups cross-functionally and randomly, rather than with intact departments or units.

Discussions with colleagues from other departments helps broaden perspective and creates a stronger sense of the company as a total team. Here's a simple technique for composing groups cross-functionally and randomly.

- Count the total number of participants in the meeting, say, 248.
- Divide that number by the number of discussants you want in the group, say, 8; thus, 248 divided by 8 is 31.
- Ask participants to count from 1 to 31.
- Ask all the 1s to meet in a certain area, the 2s to meet in a certain area, and so on until you have assigned all the groups to a meeting location.

Some of the questions generated in Step 6 will be tough to answer. Don't duck, evade, or distort.

Answer as candidly as possible. Both the facilitator and management must clearly communicate that all questions are important and none will be evaded. If you need time to track down the answer to a question, say so and follow up in a newsletter, through e-mail, through voice mail, or on a company bulletin board. Before the meeting prepare honest answers to the toughest questions that could be asked (e.g., Will there be any more layoffs?).

Management's messages to employees and answers to questions could come from a single spokesperson or a management team.

We've seen individuals represent management, and we've seen teams do the job. Your choice depends on you, your team, and your needs. If you entrust these tasks to one person, that person should be none other than the highest-ranking officer in the company.

If your company has an EAP (Employee Assistance Program), stress its importance and availability.

Having access to confidential professional counseling is an integral adjunct to Aftermath. Companies with EAPs find that a surge of activity follows downsizing. Some of your people may need emotional and psychological support to help cope. If your company does not have an EAP, contact your local mental health agency for information on starting one.

6 TOOLS FOR GROWTH

•CEO• MANAGER YOU

Customer Focus

Resources needed:

None

Tools to consult:

Envision
Culture Print
Great Expectations
Team Builder
Meeting Leader
Salary 101
Appraise for Success
Performance Pay
Whiner Cup
Team Links
One-Finger Questions

What Problem Does Customer Focus Solve?

- Our employees need to practice exceptional customer service more consistently

What Is the Aim of This Tool?

A manager we know was on a long flight on one of America's largest commercial airlines. As the food-service wagon was gradually pushed back toward his row, a less than enticing aroma filled the cabin. When an unrecognizable entrée was put on the tray table of the person to his left, he asked the flight attendant, "What is it?"

She answered flatly, "Chicken."

"Is there a choice?"

"Yes, you can eat it or you can leave it."

Do you think that airline has customer focus? Do you believe it is led by a management team that reinforces the notion that customers are a precious commodity?

What would your employees do in a situation like the one faced by the flight attendant? Are your employees so intensely focused on customer needs that they endear themselves to even the most unhappy customers, or does their focus on their own needs alienate far more customers than they win over? The premise of this tool is that you prefer the former over the latter and the tool shows you how to get it.

How Does Customer Focus Work?

This tool proposes a series of actions that when taken together represent truly exceptional customer service. Some of these actions you won't need because they are already standard practice within your company. Others may not be so appropriate to what you do for your customers. The gems for you will be the behaviors that provide your employees with a Customer Focus that keeps your clients coming back for more.

Step 1: Take the "Customer Focus Test."

Score the test which begins below for your company, department, or team, using the key to rate your level of agreement with the statements, to see which principles of exceptional customer service represent your best targets of opportunity for improvement. You may want to take this test privately, but it will be of greater value for you to take it with a group of people whose joint goal is to intensify Customer Focus.

Customer Focus Test

5 : Strongly agree 4 : Agree 3 : Slightly agree 2 : Slightly disagree 1 : Disagree 0 : Strongly disagree
NA : Not applicable to our business

___ 1. We have an ambitious, inspiring, widely known, and widely accepted customer service vision statement. It makes a clear declaration of how we value our customers as well as how we pledge to serve them.

___ 2. Management walks the customer service talk. It fully supports employee efforts to provide exceptional customer service and to realize the customer service vision of the company.

___ 3. We go out of our way to hire customer service providers who are emotionally, culturally, and intellectually prepared to provide the nature and the quality of customer service our customers expect and deserve.

___ 4. Our new employees are thoroughly oriented to our customer service culture. We baptize them with the waters of the customer service vision before we turn them loose on customers.

___ 5. Our employees receive clear statements of expectations for the kind of customer service performance we insist upon in fulfillment of the customer service vision. As a result, they know just how to handle customer service situations as they arise.

___ 6. Our employees are fully trained in all aspects of their work and especially in how to meet the expectations we have for their customer service performance.

___ 7. We treat our employees so well, and lead them with such thoughtfulness, inspiration, and compassion that they act as our *partners* to provide exceptional customer service rather than as *hired hands* just going through the motions to earn their pay. In other words, we give them good reasons to have emotional ownership of our customer service goals.

___ 8. We hold employees *accountable* for achieving our expectations for their customer service performance. They receive periodic performance reviews and other forms of abundant feedback, both positive and negative, that help them stay on track.

___ 9. We embark on continuous customer service improvement. We practically beg our employees for their ideas on how we can serve customers better and faster. We listen to those ideas and we use the ones that work.

___ 10. On the telephone and in person, our employees use language and behavior that bond them to our customers, and they avoid language and behavior that might offend customers or put them off.

___ 11. We don't allow customers to ask more than once for what they need before we swing into action to give it to them. As soon as any employee learns of a customer need, that employee feels personally responsible to see that it is met.

___ 12. Our customers don't have to lift a finger to get exceptional service. We make the call, fill out the form, check the records, correct the mistake, and otherwise go the extra mile to keep them happy.

___ 13. Customer complaints are resolved quickly, responsively, competently, happily, generously, and remorsefully, if we made an error. When we don't get it right the first time, we make sure we get it right—even *more* than right, when possible—the second time.

___ 14. We serve our internal customers as professionally, as responsively, and as faithfully as we serve our external customers. Our various departments and divisions meet each other's needs quickly and fully.

___ 15. We act every day as though we are on the verge of losing each of our customers. As a result we treat them warmly, courteously, and appreciatively. We *treasure* them.

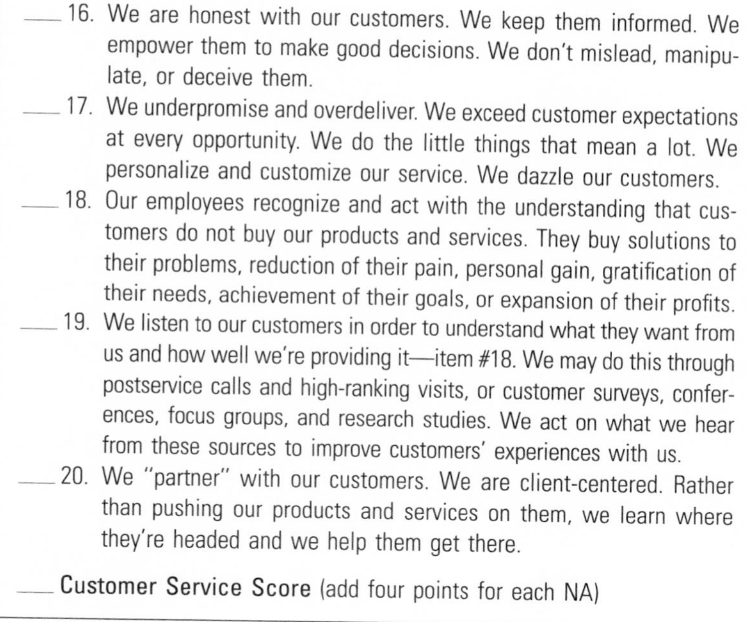

____ 16. We are honest with our customers. We keep them informed. We empower them to make good decisions. We don't mislead, manipulate, or deceive them.

____ 17. We underpromise and overdeliver. We exceed customer expectations at every opportunity. We do the little things that mean a lot. We personalize and customize our service. We dazzle our customers.

____ 18. Our employees recognize and act with the understanding that customers do not buy our products and services. They buy solutions to their problems, reduction of their pain, personal gain, gratification of their needs, achievement of their goals, or expansion of their profits.

____ 19. We listen to our customers in order to understand what they want from us and how well we're providing it—item #18. We may do this through postservice calls and high-ranking visits, or customer surveys, conferences, focus groups, and research studies. We act on what we hear from these sources to improve customers' experiences with us.

____ 20. We "partner" with our customers. We are client-centered. Rather than pushing our products and services on them, we learn where they're headed and we help them get there.

____ **Customer Service Score** (add four points for each NA)

Step 2: Grade your "Customer Focus Test."

Score	Grade	Comments
96–100	A+	Your company will have your own chapter in the next great customer service book.
90–95	A	Your company is a model for corporate America to follow.
86–89	B+	Your customers must love to deal with you.
80–85	B	Your customers must be pleased with your treatment of them.
76–79	C+	This is solid, but not great, customer service with opportunity for gain.
70–75	C	This isn't too shabby a score, but one with lots of opportunity for gain.
66–69	D+	This is a shabby score; opportunity for gain is immense.
60–65	D	You're bordering on customer abuse.
0–59	F	Your customers must need you badly to be still sticking around.

Step 3: Fill out the "Customer Focus Test Scoring Chart."
Transfer your scores on the test to the "score" box in the chart below. For items scored 0, 1, 2 or 3, what actions will you take to intensify your customer focus? You may choose to follow our suggestions or, better yet, encourage the employees who take this test to invent and agree upon their own actions.

Customer Focus Test Scoring Chart

Score Item #	A Few Suggestions	Your Ideas
#1 [ ]	■ Draft a service vision statement. (See *Envision*.) ■ Revise the current statement. ■ Get employee feedback on the worth of the current statement.	
#2 [ ]	■ Seek employee/customer opinions on how well the talk is walked. ■ Get top management support for insistence upon a better walk.	
#3 [ ]	■ Screen job candidates for those who smile, show a history of team play, fit in to your customer-care culture, and who otherwise demonstrate the desire to serve.	
#4 [ ]	■ Create a *Culture Print*. ■ Create a new employee orientation curriculum that imprints the customer culture on them; begin it during the hiring process.	

#5
- Write expectations for each employee. (See *Great Expectations*.)
- Better: Let employees take the first crack at writing the customer service expectations they ought to be held accountable for.

#6
- Initiate a customer service training curriculum.

#7
- Train managers to lead and to build and sustain high-performance teams. (See *Team Builder* and *Meeting Leader*.)
- Move all employees closer to the customer. Take them on sales calls; tell them how their output is used.
- Open the books; share the profits. (See *Performance Pay* and *Salary 101*.)

#8
- Create a performance review system that measures employee success on meeting customer service expectations and focuses on strategies for improvement. (See *Appraise for Success*.)

#9
- Find out why ideas have been scarce.
- Ask for one "I think we should . . ." note per week per employee.
- Pay employees for great ideas. (See *Performance Pay*.)

#10
- Establish a *Whiner Cup.*
- Teach them the words that will bond them to customers.
- Forbid words that customers hate to hear.

#11
- Make it a customer service rule that all employees from custodian to CEO assume personal responsibility for each customer need that comes to their attention.

#12
- Give employees specific examples of how you expect them to go beyond the call of duty in some of the most challenging customer service situations.

#13
- Train employees how to deal with angry, complaining customers.
- Empower employees to use generous make-it-right remedies.

#14
- Convince the CEO to insist upon a professipona level of service.
- Conduct yearly assessments of interdepartmental customer service quality that trigger rewards and punishment. (See *Team Links.*)
- Conduct senior-manager team building. (See *Team Builder.*)

#15 ▪ Ask your customers *One-Finger Questions.*

▪ For major accounts, assign one employee to maintain constant rapport.

#16 ▪ Disguise yourself as a customer and experience your service.

▪ Hire outside "mystery shoppers."

▪ Check signage for placement and design.

▪ Check customer instructions for clarity.

#17 ▪ Lead employee focus groups to get ideas on how to exceed employee expectations with little or no additional cost.

#18 ▪ Train employees in dealing with the specific problems, pains, pleasures, purposes, and profits you take care of for customers as well as in making certain each one is satisfied.

#19 ▪ Commit to one of these: postservice calls; high-ranking visits; or customer surveys, conferences, focus groups, and research studies.

#20 ▪ Devise a strategy to partner with your largest customers. Ask to attend their next major planning meetings.

Criticism Template

Resources needed:

None

Tools to consult:

None

What Problems Does Criticism Template Solve?

- My criticism doesn't stick; people go on doing the same thing.
- I am uncomfortable giving criticism to others.
- People get very upset when I correct their performance errors.

What Is the Aim of This Tool?

It is inevitable that you will encounter instances when employees, team members, colleagues, and even bosses fail to meet your expectations. Indeed, you may confront behavior in need of redirection almost daily. Such situations call for the delivery of constructive criticism.

Many people believe that constructive criticism is an oxymoron, a contradiction in terms. Perhaps it is because they are so often on the receiving end of criticism poorly delivered. And perhaps they too often give criticism that rarely does anything but create defensiveness and generate defiance in receivers. It doesn't have to be that way.

It *is* possible to step on people's toes without messing up their shine. This tool will teach you just how to do that. You'll learn the principles—the dos and don'ts of effective criticism. You receive an actual template you can follow in many situations. Finally, you'll get scripts for opening lines to give feedback on most of the common mistakes, slips, and failures that you see.

How Does Criticism Template Work?

The Criticism Template consists of eight steps to follow when you respond to inappropriate behavior. Not every situation calls for all of the steps, however. To show how the steps work, we've provided an example of a situation calling for criticism. A new receptionist has just arrived 35 minutes late on the first day of the third week on the job. This employee has previously been 5 minutes late on two occasions, without comment from you. As you read the steps, think about a specific criticism opportunity that *you* might encounter. After each example statement, write in what you might say in that situation.

Step 1: Identify the problem.

Before you speak, get rid of your anger. If you feel the need to punish, to get even, or to assert your authority, that's exactly what you'll do, and you will likely get an angry reaction from the recipient of your anger. But don't take too long to calm down. The closer in time that you deliver criticism to the event that triggered it, the better. The longer you wait, the less meaning it will have to the recipient, and the longer you wait, the more likely you are to change your mind: "Oh, I guess what happened really wasn't so bad."

Tell the person what event, behavior, or performance concerns you. Be specific and give examples. Focus on what happened rather than on what the person did. Follow the time-honored advice of saying what you see. One of the best ways to condemn the deed and not the doer is to begin your reproach by talking about something you observed, you heard, or that came to your attention. Don't be judgmental, and don't accuse ("You don't *want* to do a good job, do you?"). Push the word "you" as far back in your statement as possible; never let it be the first word out of your mouth. "I" and "we" are far better opening pronouns.

Receptionist example: "I noticed that the front desk wasn't covered this morning until nine thirty-five."

Step 2: Say what's wrong with the behavior.

Tell the person exactly why the event, behavior, or performance creates a problem for the organization, for the team, for customers, or for you. Give a specific impact statement. If you've already made this point to the employee, this step may not be needed.

Find a private location to say this. Never make the mistake of embarrassing employees in front of customers, peers, or others. They may eventually forgive you, but they will never forget the hurt.

Receptionist example: "When the desk isn't covered during business hours, we have customers and other visitors coming in who get a negative first impression of our attentiveness to them."

Step 3: Say how you feel.

Give your personal reaction to the situation, or describe how what happened violated a core value of the organization. Make clear how important the violation was.

Receptionist example: "We take very seriously the obligation we have to the people we serve, and I get very disappointed when we don't fulfill that obligation.

Step 4: Ask questions.

Ask the person to explain anything you may misunderstand or to offer clarifications you should hear. Don't proceed until you are sure you have the facts straight. (Some managers choose to begin with this step, especially if the recipient already understands the importance of the points they would make by going through Steps 1 through 3.)

Receptionist example: "What happened this morning?"

Step 5: Plan corrective action.

Depending on the employee's answer to your question, you may be ready to direct the discussion to a solution of the problem. It would be best to get the employee to suggest the remedy. If this has been a chronic problem, state the consequences of a recurrence. Don't make it sound like a threat unless that is your intent, and never make an *empty* threat—one you have no intent to carry through.

Focus on the behavior that the situation demands. Your goal is not to criticize, but to bring about changed behavior. This means you may be able to achieve your goal by asking for what is required rather than pointing to what the person did wrong.

Receptionist example: "We need to have you here at nine o'clock Monday through Friday. What's it going to take to make that happen consistently?"

Step 6: Get a commitment to improved performance.

Ask for a pledge to corrective action. Insist upon a "Yes, I will." Don't accept "I'll try," "Maybe I could . . . ," or "I'll do my best."

RECEPTIONIST EXAMPLE: "Taking the earlier bus every morning sounds like a good solution. Are you committed to it?"

Step 7: Give a positive stroke.

Depending on what's appropriate to your relationship, you may choose to say how you value, appreciate, or accept the person. You might also praise some positive aspect of his or her performance. Indicate your appreciation of the employee's cooperation and your optimism for a permanent solution. In all of this, however, be careful not to play down or to negate the importance of your criticism.

RECEPTIONIST EXAMPLE: "Apart from this tardiness problem, I want you to know that I really like the sensitive way I've seen you handling our visitors and incoming phone calls. I like your plan for getting here on time, and I'm looking forward to seeing it happen."

Step 8: End it.

Ask for questions or suggestions and then end the encounter to allow your words to sink in. Don't change the subject—you might diminish the impact of the criticism. Afterward, assess the interaction. How did the person react? Did you achieve your goal? What did you do well and not so well? What will you change next time? How will you follow up to ensure corrective action is taken?

RECEPTIONIST EXAMPLE: "Do you have any questions or suggestions? If not, I'll let you get back to your desk. Thank you."

How Do I Make Criticism Template Work for Me?

The Criticism Template is a helpful guide through the criticism jungle. Even so, it doesn't answer all the problem performances you face. No two performance challenges are alike, and no single response is best in all situations. To account for some of these difficulties we suggest that you study the criticism scripts that follow. These represent "first words out of your mouth" that will get you started in the right direction when you need to criticize.

The best criticism statements contain a maximum amount of *power* and a minimum of *sting*. Power changes behavior; sting hurts. Use the statements in the chart "Some Helpful Criticism

Openers" (pages 149–150), as guides to help increase the power in your feedback while removing much of the sting. Choose the level of confrontation appropriate to the person and situation.

Don't expect miracles. No matter how sensitively, tactfully, and effectively you deliver criticism, it will probably make the other person defensive. People don't like to get the message that their performance is unacceptable, no matter how gently it is sent. Prepare yourself for defensiveness. With subordinates, it comes in several forms.

- Some employees who look for excuses not to have to do the right thing will fire "yeah-buts" at you. Remember the late receptionist? He might have said during Step 4 or later, "I try very hard to get to work on time, but public transportation just isn't reliable from my part of town." Here's a good response to that "yeah-but": "I hear you and I empathize with your transportation problem, but that's not the issue. The issue is that the front desk must be covered every morning at nine o'clock. How do we make that happen?"
- Some employees who cannot accept justified criticism will accuse you of being unfair or of picking on them. One way to handle such an accusation is through a simulated role reversal. "I'm sorry you feel that way. Let's imagine that you were me—the supervisor responsible for the success of this office. You have this situation where people who enter the office in the morning are not being treated as valued customers because the person who does such a good job of greeting them is not there early enough to do it. What would *you* do?" Chances are the employee will have nothing to say. If the employee makes an unreasonable suggestion, point out why it is unworkable. If the employee suggests a solution as good as yours, or even better, consider implementing it.
- If you are accused of being too harsh, say, "I'm sorry you see it that way, but I'm afraid my commitment to excellence makes it tough for me to soft-pedal such a vital matter." If upon second thought you agree with the employee, go for a slightly less intense approach the next time.

Whatever form defensiveness to your criticism may take, what's more important is the long-term reaction. What does the initial defensiveness you get typically turn into—defiance or compliance? If you appear to be alienating people over the long haul, change your criticism to a more subtle form. If your current form of feedback is working, as shown by eventual compliance, stick with it.

Some Helpful Criticism Openers

Situation	Poor Statements	Good Subtle Statements	Good Direct Statements
Boss assigns more work than you can complete by the deadline.	That's an unreasonable request! You know I can't get this done on time!	Which of my current priorities should I put aside? Is it okay if I delay the project I'm working on now?	Given my current workload, I'm afraid I won't be able to do a quality job on that. I can't meet that deadline, but I can have it ready by . . .
Boss told you to do something one way yesterday and a different way today.	Make up your mind! You're trying to confuse me.	I must have misunderstood you yesterday. This isn't how I thought you wanted that done.	The directions I got yesterday were different. This isn't the way you asked me to do it yesterday.
Peer hasn't done his or her part on a joint project.	You're unreliable. You had no intention of getting that done on time, did you?	What can I do to help make sure we get that done on time in the future? What happened to that section of the report?	Because I didn't get your section of the report on time the project is late. I feel let down.
Peer made you look bad in front of the boss.	You tried to make me look bad in front of the boss. Why are you out to get me?	I'm very unhappy about what happened in the staff meeting this morning. Is there a reason why you said that to the boss?	I will not tolerate anyone telling the boss such a thing. Let's talk about what it's going to take to make sure that that never happens again.

Subordinate is doing a job inefficiently.	Can't anyone do anything right around here? Who told you to do it that way!?	Let me suggest a different way to handle that. I need your help with something.	Let me show you how I need to have that done. Don't do it that way; do it this way.
Subordinate neglected a customer.	You need to clean up your act. If you want to keep your job, you'll never let me catch you doing that to a customer again.	Is there a good reason why that customer was not served immediately? I just witnessed an example of poor customer service that I thought only our competition was providing.	When I see a customer being ignored like that, I get very unhappy. Customers *must* get better attention than what I just observed.

Change It

Resources needed:

None

Tools to consult:

Gripe Session
Envision
Sell It
Tactical Planner

What Problem Does Change It Solve?

- We get too much resistance to and too little cooperation with the changes we implement.
- The next time I implement change, how can I do a better job introducing it than the last time?

What Is the Aim of This Tool?

Change is buffeting American companies from many directions. Nine factors account for most of this change.

1. Productivity. The never-ending demand for employees to do more, do it better, and do it cheaper.
2. Technology. Every time we turn around there's a new computer to get used to, a software upgrade to learn, and a job no longer needed.
3. Reengineering. Just when we think we know what it takes to get ahead, the rules change—from one hierarchical configuration to another, from one leadership style to another, from one process for serving customers to another.
4. Societal expectations. The definition of social responsibility remains in constant flux. Each time that definition shifts, organizational priorities shift along with it.

5. **Diversity.** In many parts of this country the workforce still looks the way it did 50 years ago. For many employees, the first time they work alongside someone who doesn't look like them, dress like them, sound like them, or think like them is traumatic.
6. **Workforce.** Apart from diversity issues, each new generation of employees brings new challenges, especially in terms of work ethic, desire for life-work balance, and academic preparation.
7. **Market demands.** Customers grow more educated, more discriminating, and more difficult to please.
8. **Regulation.** The legal and regulatory landscape grows more complex and more constraining.
9. **Competition.** There's a danger in being number one. You're the standard that all others have in their sights. You can't afford to become intoxicated with your own success and grow complacent.

Whatever the circumstances that force a company to change, change is typically introduced to the workforce by top management. The manner of that introduction will have much to do with how well the change is accepted and implemented. Change It shows you how to realize change with a minimum of resistance and a maximum of cooperation.

The Chinese ideogram (word picture) for change has two parts: the first signifies "threat"; the second signifies "opportunity." The next time you implement change, don't focus only on opportunity and lose sight of the threat. This change you're pushing through is going to scare some employees. The better you can empathize with that fright, the better you will be able to reduce it. The more you can reduce it, the more successful you are going to be in realizing the advantages of the change.

How Does Change It Work?

The purpose of the "Change It Test" opposite is to help you assess how effectively you minimize the resistance that others experience when you are in the driver's seat implementing change.

Step 1: Take the "Change It Test."

Consider a specific change you recently introduced, or are currently introducing, to employees, or one that another level of management has initiated and that you observed. Describe the change in the space provided at the top of the chart. Then rate your level of agreement with the statements.

Change It Test

The change I'm assessing: ______________________________

____

5 : Strongly agree 4 : Agree 3 : Slightly agree
2 : Slightly disagree 1 : Disagree 0 : Strongly disagree
NA : Not applicable

____ 1. We shared our vision for the future that this change was intended to help us create. As a result employees knew exactly what we hoped to accomplish and why.

____ 2. We kept employees closely connected to customers, competitors, and other environmental factors so they weren't shocked by the need for change in response to those factors.

____ 3. We involved them up front in determining the need for the change and in deciding how to respond to that need.

____ 4. Once the nature of the change was identified, we involved them in planning for its implementation.

____ 5. We anticipated the losses employees would feel, the threat they would experience, and the objections they would have to the change. We took these losses, threats, and objections into account as the plan took shape.

____ 6. We explained the change clearly and completely to all who would be affected by it. They knew what to expect, in both the short and long term.

____ 7. We let people vent their frustrations, either one-on-one or in organized gripe sessions. We answered them objectively and nondefensively; we countered wild rumors with honest information.

____ 8. We validated their fears and concerns; we were patient with their reluctance.

____ 9. We demonstrated how the change would benefit both the organization and employees.

____ 10. We did what we could to include visible benefits in the change for employees.

____ 11. We demonstrated our commitment to the change by the resources (e.g., funds, equipment, materials, staffing, training) we committed to it.

____ 12. Throughout the process we remained upbeat and expressed our optimism about its success.

____ 13. We made certain that a well-thought-out action plan for implementation was formulated and followed.

Step 2: Score your test.

Add up the scores you gave to the items in this test. If you left any items blank, assign to them as a score the average of the other scores.

ENTER YOUR SCORE HERE: ________

Step 3: Grade your test.

"Scoring the Change It Test" will give you some idea of how effectively the change you identified was implemented.

Scoring the Change It Test

Score	Grade	Implication
63–65	A+	You're a terrific change agent!
58–62	A	You're doing about everything you can to garner support for change.
56–57	B+	You're doing a much better job than most to reduce resistance to change.
51–55	B	You're doing a better job than most to reduce resistance to change.
49–50	C+	While there's room for improvement, you're an okay change agent.
44–48	C	This is no worse than many managers, but you can do better.
42–43	D+	Expect resistance to the changes you introduce.
37–41	D	Expect stiff resistance to the changes you introduce.
0–36	F	Expect rebellion!

Step 4: Plan for improvements.

Circle the test items on which you scored lower than 4. These are your targets of opportunity for betterment in the way you initiate change. For each one—and especially for the ones that scored lowest—answer these questions:

- What factors contribute to making this such a poorly practiced item?
- How can the poorly practiced factors be reversed to enable you do to a better job the next time you launch change?
- What's your specific plan for improvement?

How Do I Make Change It Work for Me?

Try these suggestions for getting the greatest mileage out of the "Change It Test":

- Give a blank copy of the test to the employees who were most affected by the change you rated. Have them score it for comparison to your perception of your (or management's) actions as change agents. Discuss contrasting perceptions with those employees.
- Use the test to give superiors feedback on their shortcomings when it comes to implementing change.
- Use the test as the outline of a seminar or a checklist for managers in your company to use the next time they implement change.

Gripe Session

Resources needed:

Flip chart
Markers
¾-inch colored sticky dots
Meeting room

Tools to consult:

Change It
Lead with Your Ears

What Problems Does Gripe Session Solve?

- My managers and I are starving for some honest feedback from our employees.
- Our people have a great deal of pent-up anger and hostility. How can we vent it constructively and move forward as a team?
- Employees aren't sending good news, bad news, or great news up the line.

What Is the Aim of This Tool?

A consultant was asked into an engineering company to provide leadership training. In a meeting with top management, the vice president for human resources said, "As you train our people, there are a number of issues we hope you will not address. One in particular is the performance review. We've just implemented a new system that has upset them, and we prefer that you not stir them up further."

The consultant was amazed. He thought to himself that top management might just as well have reacted by decreeing that no more than two employees were allowed to congregate in the hallways for fear of organized rebellion. He asked the vice president if management had considered conducting a Gripe Session where employees might vent their frustrations with the performance review plan.

The consultant had pushed the wrong button. Trying to control his anger, the vice president fired back, "You may be a good consultant, but your lack of management experience shows. Do you realize what will happen if we open ourselves to employees on this matter? All they'll do is moan, grumble, and complain!"

"I hope so—that's the whole idea" was the consultant's response. He went on to point out that managers must be ready to suffer the slings and arrows of outrageous complaints for two reasons: First, it is better to bear these attacks in the open, where you can see them and address them. Second, when you really listen, you may discover that a few of the concerns aren't as outrageous as you originally thought.

A well-conducted Gripe Session may be just what your team or company needs to overcome barriers standing in its way. It will also give management valuable feedback on the impact its decisions are having on employees.

How Does Gripe Session Work?

Eventually, the vice president for human resources asked the consultant for his advice on convening a Gripe Session. Here are the consultant's prescriptions.

Step 1: Announce the session.

Tell employees you want to get their ideas on the new performance review process. Try to limit each scheduled session to 20 employees to increase the likelihood that each person will say something. Don't label the meeting a "gripe session."

Step 2: Pose the right question.

Say something like "We are here because I am at a disadvantage. I've heard concerns about the new performance review plan, but I don't have as clear a statement from you as I need. The only way I can respond intelligently and satisfactorily is to know your precise needs and expectations. The only way we can make this review process work better for us to is to be honest about how it's working right now. So please share your concerns with me. It may help you to do that by answering the question 'What's one thing you would change to improve the new performance review system?' " By asking how something can be improved, rather than what's wrong with it, you start the meeting moving in a constructive direction.

Step 3: Promise a response, not repercussions.

After you ask your question, guarantee participants that their input to the meeting will be seen as positive, not negative, no matter how critical they are, as long as the criticism is given in the spirit of making things better. See that your subordinate managers *fulfill* this pledge following the meeting!

Step 4: Record their answers.

For this purpose a flip chart has several advantages over other data collection methods. Participants can see all that is said, which encourages them to build on the ideas of their colleagues. It demonstrates that you're listening and that what is being said is important to you. Most important, the permanent log it provides suggests that you plan to do something with the information you collect.

When the gripes begin to fly, *say nothing*. This is the most critical factor in your behavior at a Gripe Session. While suggestions are being made and concerns are being aired, limit your speaking to clarification questions ("Are you saying that . . . ?"). If you were to give your unbridled reactions to what you hear at this time, some of those reactions would almost certainly be defensive and possibly punitive. This action, or inaction, is crucial. Many a Gripe Session has been blown by a leader who showed anger.

Step 5: Prioritize their suggestions.

Once the list is complete, get the group to vote for the suggestions they believe are most important. This will tell you where to focus your response. Use sticky dots for the vote. Give each person a number of dots equal to about one third of the total number of suggestions. Once they vote, lead a discussion of the results.

Step 6: Invoke the 48-hour promise.

Once everything has been said, don't utter the typical and often insincere "We'll get back to you" pledge. Instead say, "I'll be in this room 48 hours from now with a response to the recommendations you have made." The 48-hour promise proves you're serious. It give you the opportunity you may need to get over any hurt feelings, to cool down, and to see things from the perspective of employees. And it has you getting back to them so quickly that they won't expect the miraculous cures they would hope for if you took 48 days instead.

Step 7: Thank them.

Your employees may feel they've gone out on a limb in being honest with you. Tell them how pleased you are that they have been so forthcoming and constructive with their feelings, attitudes, and opinions.

Step 8: Respond to the suggestions.

When you return to the group 48 hours later, nondefensively address their list of concerns, one by one. Follow these guidelines:

- Acknowledge that each of the points made was valid in the sense that the employees honestly felt they were important.
- Earmark the items on the list that have arisen out of miscommunication, and clear up the misunderstandings as you see them.
- Identify the suggestions that are unworkable, and say why you view them this way.
- Identify the suggestions that you believe warrant attention, either immediately or in the future, and commit to their inclusion in the performance review plan.

Involve Gripe Session participants as much as possible in the incorporation of the helpful suggestions into the plan, perhaps by asking some of them to join a focus group dedicated to the task.

Step 9: Remain accountable.

Show through your actions that valid concerns won't be ignored. Reconvene the groups in three months to check on progress and see what else needs to be done.

How Do I Make Gripe Session Work for Me?

Keep these considerations in mind as you plan your Gripe Session.

- **Plan a Gripe Session whenever employees need to vent.** The rapid change in today's work environment is causing distress for many employees. Gripe Session gives them a chance to relieve some of that distress, and it teaches you how to avoid some of the unnecessary angst you may be creating.

- **Consider various opening questions.** The question in the example was stated to generate suggestions and keep the meeting upbeat. Sometimes it will be necessary instead to focus on the pain employees are feeling. In these cases, a more appropriate form of question will be "What are the specific concerns you have about the new performance review plan?"
- **Prepare to take the heat.** Expect to hear frustration and even anger in the voices and in the words of employees. Don't get defensive when you do. If the Gripe Session is to have a positive outcome, you must see it as an opportunity to repair morale and improve productivity. This is not an occasion to defend your honor and your judgment. A gripe session represents catharsis, not crisis.
- **What if no one says anything?** Your opening question could be met with blank stares. You may have to get the ball rolling. One way to do this is to propose to the group a list of improvements you believe they will suggest, and ask them to begin the session by voting for those they feel are most needed. You might put the seven or eight factors you think trouble them the most on a large sheet of flip-chart paper at the front of the room. You can say, "Here are a few of the concerns I've heard. Are there any you've heard from colleagues that should be added to the list before we discuss them?" Once the list is complete, ask them to come forward to place the three sticky dots on the sheet to indicate the three improvements they believe are most needed. Comment briefly on the resulting distribution of dots on the sheet and ask why they believe the top vote-getter got so many hits. This icebreaker should get them talking.

Full-Circle Growth

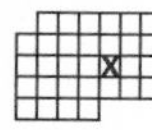

Resources needed:

Full-Circle Growth Survey

Tools to consult:

Lemons and Oranges
Great Expectations

What Problems Does Full-Circle Growth Solve?

- My managers and I are starving for some honest feedback from our employees.
- We need to do a better job of developing our people.

What Is the Aim of This Tool?

More and more companies are learning a basic truth about management effectiveness: An essential measurement of managerial capability can be found in the impact managers have on the people they serve—bosses, peers, employees, and customers. As a result, more and more managers are being given the opportunity to learn what reaction their constituencies have to their management style.

Full-Circle Growth gives a targeted group of managers feedback on the impact of their performance on subordinates, peers, superiors, and possibly other groups. The method we recommend maximizes the honesty and minimizes the threat of that feedback to both the giver and the receiver.

Unlike most so-called 360-degree feedback plans, Full-Circle Growth goes one important step further. It holds managers accountable for the feedback they receive by assisting them in the development of a comprehensive professional development plan for the coming year based on the feedback.

How Does Full-Circle Growth Work?

Full-Circle Growth is custom designed to meet the management development needs of your company. So pick and choose from among the following steps for the guidelines that will yield a management development plan that works best for you.

Step 1: Garner support for the plan.

Before you invest a significant amount of time and money into this tool, be sure you have support from all levels of the organization. Full-Circle Growth requires commitment from all involved in order to succeed. If managers can't find the time to follow through on their development plans (Step 9), much of the value of this tool will be lost.

Step 2: Assign a plan manager.

The role of the plan manager is to administer your Full-Circle Growth project, ensuring that each of the following steps are carried out. The four most important qualities for a Full-Circle Growth plan manager to possess are:

1. A high level of management and organizational skills
2. Credibility within the organization—especially with targeted managers
3. Enthusiasm for the plan
4. Enough time to dig in and make it succeed

The plan manager might be chosen from your human resources department and in any case should not be included in the plan as a participant.

Step 3: Choose the population to be assessed.

Include individuals from similar managerial levels. Don't mix executives with first-line supervisors in the same management development plan.

Step 4: Choose the population that will perform the assessments.

Assume you have chosen to target senior managers to be assessed and developed. The following checklist indicates those who may be in a position to provide those managers with valid feedback on their performance. Feedback from more than four or five sources can be difficult to digest. Whom among these would you choose to give feedback to *your* senior managers?

___ Board of directors
___ CEO
___ Other superiors
___ Peers
___ Self
___ Direct subordinates
___ Indirect subordinates
___ Internal customers
___ External customers
___ Suppliers

Step 5: Identify dimensions of performance to be measured by the "Full-Circle Growth Survey."

What do successful people who occupy the position(s) to be assessed by the survey do? Write out the behaviors you will measure. Some recommended managerial dimensions to assess are on the sample survey on pages 164–165. You may find the items on it helpful as possible items in your survey, but the sample is far from all-inclusive. You should use items that reflect the unique character of your business—feel free to change the wording.

If your final list contains fewer than 20 items, it may either be missing critical success factors or include items that are too broad to generate meaningful feedback. If your final list contains more than 50 items, it may split hairs. Longer lists also quickly become tedious for raters and discourage thoroughness. Don't be too concerned about settling on a single list of survey items that will be equally relevant for all groups that will complete the survey. Your goal with this tool is to generate helpful feedback, not to fashion a statistically defensible profile.

Sample Full-Circle Growth Survey Items

Leadership skills

- Communicates a clear and inspiring vision to his/her subordinates.
- States clearly his/her expectations for performance.
- Recognizes the efforts of others with appreciation and praise.
- Delegates responsibility; is willing to let go of the reins and trust others.

Development of others

- Is a willing mentor in the career development of others.
- Provides others with opportunities to learn and grow.
- Appraises the performance of others in a timely manner.
- Coaches and counsels staff over the rough spots and during difficult times.

Influence

- Supports his/her positions with solid evidence.
- Successfully influences the thinking of subordinates.
- Successfully influences the thinking of peers.
- Successfully influences the thinking of superiors.

Interpersonal skills

- Creates a positive working environment with others.
- Treats others with respect.
- Deals fairly with everyone; plays no favorites.
- Demonstrates tact and sensitivity in dealings with others.

Communication skills

- Listens well.
- Keeps others informed; gives them the information they need to do a good job.
- Speaks clearly, correctly, and to the point.
- Writes clearly, correctly, and to the point.

Conflict management

- Expresses disagreement constructively without being offensive or antagonistic.
- Resolves conflict with others effectively.
- Resolves conflict between others effectively.
- Is a decisive and effective disciplinarian.

Action orientation

- Monitors projects closely; takes action to resolve problems before they get out of hand.
- Brings new ideas and opportunities to the attention of the company.
- Is a self-starter; makes things happen.
- Follows through on tasks and fulfills promises; achieves goals for job performance.

Organization skills

- Makes good use of time; avoids wasting time.
- Sets personal goals for job performance.
- Establishes realistic budgets and time lines for assigned projects.
- Organizes own work in an efficient manner.

Professional growth

- Learns from his/her mistakes.
- Seeks out opportunities to learn, grow, and improve.
- Asks for feedback on his/her performance.
- Responds well to feedback received on his/her performance.

Character

- Has the courage of his/her convictions.
- Says what he/she means and means what he/she says.
- Willingly shares the spotlight with others.
- Maintains the highest ethics and moral code; demonstrates integrity and honesty.

Customer service

- Is recognized by customers as a leading service provider in the company.
- Anticipates, identifies, and resolves problems in customer relationships.
- Provides distinctive customer service; adds value to customer businesses.
- Provides subordinates with the resources they need to serve customers exceptionally.

Performance

- Demonstrates a thorough working knowledge of personal computers and appropriate software.
- Has a high degree of technical expertise in his/her field.
- Has a thorough understanding of our industry.
- Makes decisions that are rational and are based on available data.

Step 6: Create the rating scale.

Ask raters to identify the performance dimensions the person being assessed needs most to improve. One excellent way to do this is to use the *Lemons and Oranges* tool, where managers receive an equal number of lemons (least effective behaviors) and oranges (most effective behaviors) from each feedback giver. (Read *Lemons and Oranges* before proceeding with this tool.)

Step 7: Decide how you will handle confidentiality.

You may or may not choose to allow recipients of feedback to know how each rater assigned lemons and oranges. The decision will hinge on the particular leadership climate within your company. If you opt for confidentiality, take every precaution to protect it, especially as you do Steps 8, 9, and 10.

Step 8: Distribute "Full-Circle Growth Surveys."

Send the survey to as many people in each group who are willing to complete it. There is little need to limit the size of the rating population, except to ensure that they know the subject well enough to provide ratings based on personal experience rather than hearsay. Don't overburden any one rater with an excessive number of surveys—10 or 12 are probably tops. Give raters a deadline of about one week to complete their surveys.

Step 9: Collect and analyze "Full-Circle Growth Surveys."

Be prepared to execute this step quickly and accurately. You shouldn't need the help of a computer. Good, old-fashioned hand scoring of the lemons and oranges should work fine.

Step 10: Reveal feedback results to recipients.

Use a format similar to the survey itself to report the data to those who were surveyed. Array the data like the "Sample Feedback Chart" opposite, to make it easy for recipients to understand the feedback. Note that the actual chart you create will have as many rows as the number of items in the survey. The count of lemons and oranges in each of the four scoring columns will be equal if feedback givers have followed the instructions and give each feedback recipient the stipulated, and equal, number of each. You would not expect the number of lemons and oranges in each row to be equal. The distribution (clustering) of lemons and

Sample Feedback Chart

L = Lemons O = Oranges

	Self	Subordinates	Peers	Superiors	Survey Items
L					1. Communicates a clear and inspiring vision to her subordinates.
O	1	2	4	1	
L	1	6	1	2	2. States clearly her expectations for performance.
O		1			
L				2	3. Recognizes the efforts of others with appreciation and praise.
O		7			

oranges across the rows draws attention to the survey items that represent either strengths (preponderance of oranges) or development needs (preponderance of lemons) in the management behavior of the feedback recipient.

Step 11: Assign coaches.

Each manager will have a coach, whose role is to help the receiver make sense of the feedback, decide what to do about it (growth plan), and provide encouragement along the way. The coach also helps measure progress and recommends changes in the plan as needed. The coach may be the recipient's supervisor; in some cases another manager might fulfill the role more effectively. For high-level managers, an outside consultant may be the best choice.

Step 12: Train coaches.

Once coaches have been assigned, and before they meet initially with feedback recipients, train them how to perform effectively in your particular edition of Full-Circle Growth. The basis for that training might be "Points for Coaches to Ponder," on page 168.

Points for Coaches to Ponder

- Begin the first session by going over the manager's development plan. Set the goal of helping that person feel total confidence in the plan. Ask questions to help the manager refine the plan to increase its effectiveness. Make certain the development goals are practical, attainable, and measurable.
- Establish a schedule of monthly meetings for the year, with weekly meetings in the first month. Give these sessions a high priority on your calendar. If a meeting is displaced by an urgent event of higher priority, reschedule that meeting immediately.
- Don't feel the need to play the role of expert adviser or God. Your personal experiences will be an important aspect in the coaching effort, but your role is more that of a facilitator than resident authority. Relax and help the people you coach find the answers themselves to their questions, their dilemmas, and their development needs.
- Offer your suggestions as a point of view, rather than as the final word. Try these phrases when you give advice: "Another way of looking at that is . . . "; "Have you thought of what might happen if . . . ?"; "As I see it, . . . "; "You may want to consider an alternate explanation for that"; "It appears that . . . "
- Encourage managers to focus their attention on one development area at a time.
- When you feel you might benefit from another point of view regarding a manager's situation, don't hesitate to request assistance from a colleague or from the plan manager.
- Throughout your meetings, especially the first few, emphasize your belief in the importance of management development.
- As you see your managers make progress, praise their efforts and recognize their successes. Be their cheerleader as well as their coach.
- If you see your managers fail to make progress, point this out to them with gentleness, yet with candor. You do them no favor by glossing over their weaknesses.
- Finally, your success as a coach will depend more on your honesty and your commitment than on your expertise. If you are dedicated to helping managers grow, they will sense it, appreciate it, and respond in the way we all hope.

Step 13: Have recipients write goal statements and construct growth plans.

Managers participating in this process write three to five goal statements as the direct result of the feedback analysis they perform at their coaching sessions. Consider the case of someone who received a large number of lemons on the item "Resolves conflict directly and tactfully with others." As a result of the lemons and other data, the manager might conclude that he or she too often avoids situations of disagreement. One of the goal statements he or she might emerge with is "To be more direct with my opinion at staff meetings—especially when I disagree with what's being said."

In that same person's growth plan, the conflict resolution goal might account for the following entries:

Sample Growth Plan

When	What	Why
1/15	Meet with Jan Kunkle.	To get some tips on how Jan stays so calm and yet so effectively assertive in our staff meetings.
1/19—Next staff meeting	Apologize to the staff for my previous unwillingness to be honest about my disagreement and vow to do better.	To avoid surprising or confusing them with my new behavior and to garner their support.
2/15	Complete my reading of the book *Getting to Yes.*	To become more comfortable with and knowledgeable about win-win negotiation.
3/27	Attend the seminar "Managing Conflict, Anger, and Hostility."	To gain confidence in being able to disagree honestly, and not have to worry that I'll come across antagonistically.
4/22—Staff meeting	Ask the staff if they notice any improvement.	To get specific feedback on anything else I can do to disagree effectively.

The example on page 169 suggests the kinds of activities that might go into a growth plan. Other activities include organizing a small group of managers who have identified for themselves the same goal area, listening to audio- or videotapes on the subject, and rotating to another job for a while where the manager might gain relevant experience. (You may want to provide managers with a standard form they can use to record their plans.)

Step 14: Create a training curriculum.

If your target group of managers is large enough, you may be able to justify offering a series of seminars covering the most common goal areas identified by the group.

Step 15: Assess the results of the plan and respond.

About three-fourths of the way into Full-Circle Growth, participant managers should submit a report to the plan manager describing their progress. At a meeting of all participants, each one will have ten minutes to share with others what he or she has learned. At the closing date of the plan, participants submit a final report to the plan manager along with a statement of areas where they may need additional growth. At this time, the survey is readministered to see the new distribution of lemons and oranges and perhaps to initiate a new set of goal statements and growth plans.

When You Use Full-Circle Growth Make Sure You . . .

- Limit the use of the survey data to this growth program. Do not connect it in any way to performance evaluation. Participants will be far more open to changing their behavior if they are confident that the results of the survey will in no way be used against them.
- Provide feedback to managers within one month of collecting survey data. Keep the process moving. Don't allow the process to get bogged down by running the program concurrently with a busy season in your business or some other distraction.
- Encourage participant managers to follow up with raters regarding any puzzling feedback before they write the goal statements that lead to growth plans. Although the responses of individual raters should remain confidential, you might permit

receivers to query them, either individually or in a group setting, in this fashion: "While I gave myself an orange as a listener, three of the people who report to me gave lemons. That tells me they're seeing something in me of which I'm not aware. Do you have any idea what behavior they see that I'm apparently blind to?"

Performance Fixer

Resources needed:

None

Tools to consult:

Appraise for Success
Great Expectations
Lead with Your Ears
Performance Pay
Gripe Session
Team Links
Team Builder
Hero Table

What Problem Does Performance Fixer Solve?

- I have a problem performer on my hands.

What Is the Aim of This Tool?

Suppose you brought your car to a mechanic and without asking you any questions about the car or checking any of its systems he told you that it needed a new transmission. Or suppose you went to an internist and without asking you any questions or checking any of your systems she told you that you needed an operation. What would you think? Probably that you were dealing with a mechanic who was a crook and a physician who was a quack. Any professional knows that before you fix a problem you have to diagnose the problem.

Yet we are amazed at the number of intelligent, insightful managers who will act on gut-level hunches when it comes to people problems. These managers are smart enough to know that fixing an expensive machine would require more than educated guesswork. Yet they try to fix their most valuable resource, people, precisely that way.

With Performance Fixer your guesswork, biases, and assumptions will be replaced with logic, data, and objectivity. You will begin to solve people problems with the same analytical rigor you use to fix machines, with increasingly effective results.

How Does Performance Fixer Work?

This tool is a diagnostic checklist for determining the most likely cause and possible solutions for an employee's poor performance. After answering a series of questions, you'll have a clearer understanding of the underlying causes of a performance problem and be in a better position to solve it. The checklist is based on a simple formula,

$$\text{Performance} = f\,(\text{Ability}) \times (\text{Effort}) \times (\text{Resources})$$

This means that employee performance is a function of (i.e., is related to) the multiplied effects of three factors:

Ability: The talent, skill, and knowledge necessary for the task. *Can* the employee do the job?

Effort: The motivation and commitment the task requires. *Will* the employee do the job?

Resources: Organizational and managerial support (time, materials, information, money, equipment) necessary for the task. *Could* the employee do the job?

Total performance is determined by multiplying rather than adding the three factors. Stated differently, if the value of any of the three factors is zero, performance will be zero, regardless of the magnitude of the other three factors. Intuition confirms this logic. If an employee has zero ability, performance will also be zero, regardless of how hard the person works. Similarly, if effort or resources are zero, performance will be zero regardless of how skillful the employee is.

When an employee fails to meet your expectations, the reason might be that the employee *can't do it* (ability), *won't do it* (effort), or *couldn't do it* (resources). How can you be sure which one it is? The Performance Fixer answers the question.

Step 1: Review your expectations.

Think about an employee whose current performance is not meeting your expectations. Answer the following question: *Have you told the employee in clear, unequivocal, and direct language that he or she is not meeting your expectations?*

If your answer is no, have that conversation today. Do not go on to Step 2A. Why would an employee fix something he or she doesn't know is broken?

If the answer to this question is *yes,* continue with Step 2A.

Step 2A: Run Stage 1 of the "Performance Fixer Diagnostic."

The questions on our "Performance Fixer Diagnostic" call for a *yes* or *no* response. For some of the questions you may have trouble selecting either *yes* or *no*. Use your best judgment and the best information available to you.

Performance Fixer Diagnostic—Stage 1: Ability

Diagnostic Questions	Yes	No
1. Has the employee ever successfully demonstrated proficiency at this job, for you or another employer?	___	___
2. Has the employee ever passed a performance-based proficiency test either during preemployment screening or while on the job?	___	___
3. Has the nature of the job significantly changed in terms of the skills and talent required to perform it?	___	___

INTERPRETATION: If you checked the three questions in Stage 1 in a *yes-yes-no* sequence, you can rule out lack of ability as the source of the problem. This means you have an effort or resource problem. Any other sequence suggests an ability problem.

Step 2B: If you have diagnosed an ability (can't do) problem, here are several possible responses.

Recommend for this employee:

- One-on-one job coaching by the supervisor
- Apprenticeship program with a successful employee
- Classroom or on-the-job training
- Reassignment to others of most difficult duties
- Transfer to a less difficult position
- Termination

To avoid future problems with other employees, carry out:

- More careful selection and recruitment
- Improved employee testing
- More comprehensive orientation

- Job training matched to job requirements
- Closer monitoring of employee physical/emotional states.

Step 3A: Run Stage 2 of the "Performance Fixer Diagnostic."

Performance Fixer Diagnostic—Stage 2: Effort

Diagnostic Questions	Yes	No
4. Has the employee complained to you and others about being underpaid as compared to coworkers?	___	___
5. Has the employee complained to you or others about being overworked as compared to coworkers?	___	___
6. Has the employee complained to you about any working conditions, such as coworkers, safety, or equipment, that are bothersome, annoying, or frustrating?	___	___
7. Has any recent major change in corporate policy—say, compensation—created controversy and led to employee complaints?	___	___
8. Is the employee aware of any impending changes, such as mergers, acquisitions, reengineering, or downsizing, that might threaten his or her job security?	___	___
9. Given the employee's past interpersonal behavior, does he or she seem more withdrawn, moody, and depressed and less sociable than usual?	___	___

INTERPRETATION: If the answers to all the Stage 2 questions are *no*, you can probably rule out effort as the root problem. Go to Step 4A. If you answered *yes* to any question, proceed to Step 3B.

Step 3B: Consider the following options for an effort (won't do) problem.

- Interview the employee and just listen.
- Implement *Lead with Your Ears.*
- Coach and counsel the employee.
- Implement *Appraise for Success.*
- Refer employee for professional counseling.
- Make sure compensation is equitable, internally (within the company) and externally (in the marketplace).
- Conduct an employee attitude survey.

- Implement *Performance Pay.*
- Renegotiate employee's compensation package.
- Implement *Gripe Session.*

Step 4A: Run Stage 3 of the "Performance Fixer Diagnostic."

Performance Fixer Diagnostic—Stage 3: Resources

Diagnostic Questions	Yes	No
10. Does the employee have the proper tools to perform the job?	___	___
11. Is the employee working with quality materials?	___	___
12. Are you sure the employee knows the level and the degree of quality expected?	___	___
13. Is the employee given sufficient time to perform the job?	___	___
14. Is the employee given sufficient training to perform the job?	___	___
15. Is the employee receiving helpful cooperation and assistance from other employees?	___	___
16. Is the employee receiving consistent leadership and responsive coaching from superiors?	___	___

INTERPRETATION: If you answered *no* to any of the questions in Stage 3, you may have a resource problem. Proceed to Step 4B.

Step 4B: Consider these suggestions for a resource (couldn't do) problem.

- Upgrade tools and equipment.
- Set goals that are challenging yet achievable.
- Implement *Team Links.*
- Implement *Team Builder.*
- Implement *Great Expectations.*
- Implement *Hero Table.*
- Examine the quality of training programs.
- Closely examine the quality of supervision and management in the company. Do not expect positive attitudes to result from oppressive or inconsistent leadership.
- Train managers in coaching and counseling skills.
- Remove bottlenecks that may reduce the employee's performance.

How Do I Make Performance Fixer Work for Me?

Don't make the mistake of labeling all performance problems as "attitude" problems.

The message of this tool is very clear. Some problems are *can't do*, some are *won't do*, some are *couldn't do*, and some are a combination of all three. Rule out *can't do* and *couldn't do* before you accept *won't do*.

Stop telling people to "work harder."

Perhaps the most important lesson of this tool is that telling people to make a greater effort is futile if they do not have the requisite abilities or resources. You're far more likely to alienate than to motivate with this request.

Use the "Performance Fixer Diagnostic" during employee coaching and counseling sessions.

The diagnostic provides a structured agenda for a coaching and counseling session with an employee. You might even give the employee a copy of the questions and ask him or her to answer them prior to the session. For example, your perceptions of resources provided may differ from the employee's perceptions. This tool gives you the opportunity to clear up such misperceptions.

One-Day Retreat

Resources needed:

Whistle
Meeting room for 15–30 people
Three breakout rooms

Tools to consult:

Vista
Strategic Planner
Tactical Planner

What Problems Does One-Day Retreat Solve?

- We need to figure out better ways of doing things around here.
- Team members aren't on the same wavelength; they don't mesh as they should.
- We need more teamwork in this company, from top to bottom.
- We need better communication throughout the company.

What Is the Aim of This Tool?

Jeff Bracker, one of our colleagues and a nationally renowned expert on entrepreneurship, once observed that a retreat is misnamed. It should really be called an "advance." Although his observation is based on wordplay, the underlying logic is insightful. The reasons teams meet off-site are to recharge their batteries, renew their focus, and help the company move forward.

Sports teams attend preseason training camps away from their home city. These camps not only provide an opportunity for athletes to get back into condition and learn plays, they also develop team cohesiveness. At these camps players leave the real world behind and for an intense period focus on becoming a team. They practice, eat, sleep, and play together. By "retreating" to a camp they move forward in building a potential championship season.

You can gain the same advantages for your company or team. By getting your people away from the daily grind, you can improve the ease of communication between them, the understanding they have of each other, and the commitment they feel toward the goals they all share.

One-Day Retreat is not a long-range planning meeting or a strategic planning session. (See *Strategic Planner* and *Tactical Planner*.) You and your colleagues are not in seclusion to plan the future direction and strategy of the company. On the contrary, the One-Day Retreat assumes that the mission and vision have already been established. Rather, the purpose of this tool is to reenergize the group, sharpen their focus on the future, and tap into the creative juices of the team.

There are two keys to implementing this tool. The first is to establish an exciting and informative agenda. When your team walks away at the end of the day they will feel . . .

- Energized
- More focused on goals
- Happier about working with the team
- A sense of accomplishment
- Increased commitment to the team

The second key is the magic number three: three management topics, three creative assignments, and three breakout groups. These three threes provide maximum coverage with maximum group participation, all in a single day.

How Does One-Day Retreat Work?

Step 1: Define the group that will participate.

The type of agenda we suggest in Step 3 works best for groups with 15 to 30 members. If the number of people at your retreat is less than 15, the breakout groups will be too small. If the total size is larger than 30, create additional discussion groups. You can invite to the retreat a whole department (a vertical slice of the organization), a certain level of management (horizontal slice), or the total organization.

Step 2: Choose an off-site facility with ample space for group discussions.

Most hotels and conference centers provide the space you will need. We do not recommend you conduct the retreat on-site. Advise participants to turn off beepers and leave laptop computers in the office.

Step 3: Create an agenda.

Divide the day into two halves. The morning will reconnect the team with the goals of the company, the major issues facing them, and changes they should monitor. Design the afternoon to be a little more playful and entertaining while still focusing on teamwork and company goals. Each of the following steps contains an agenda component you can revise as appropriate and assemble into a master agenda for your group.

Step 4: Begin the retreat with a speech whose goals are the same as a State of the Union address.

When the president of the United States addresses a joint meeting of the Congress each January to report on the State of the Union, the speech helps everyone in the country reconnect with the goals of the elected administration. At the retreat your leader (CEO, VP, general manager) should reconnect your team with the company goals.

The tone of this speech should be upbeat and inspirational. Keep charts and slides to a minimum. Keep in mind the idea of a half-time speech. Imagine that you are a coach talking to your team in the locker room. Motivate, renew spirits, and challenge them to do even better "in the second half."

Retreat Agenda

8:00–8:30 A.M.—"State of the Company" address

- What have been our greatest successes? How have the people in the room contributed to these successes?
- What are the most pressing problems facing us? Where are we making our greatest progress on them? What still needs to be done?
- What are the major external forces affecting us? How should we respond to them?
- What are the most exciting opportunities ahead?

Step 5: Ask appropriate managers to prepare for the three 15-minute briefings.

The tone for each of these three briefings should be dramatic and focused. Imagine that you are an assistant coach on the sidelines talking to players who have just run out of the locker room. They just heard the coach ("State of the Company" address). Now they're listening to you. The time frames are tight. Stick to them. You'll have time to answer questions and discuss details later. Use only those graphs and charts that are essential. Tell a story.

8:30–8:45 A.M.—Customer briefing: "What our external customers are telling us."

- What are our best customers saying about us?
- If we're losing customers, to whom are we losing them and why?
- How well are we retaining our customer focus?
- What can we do to help our customers serve their customers better?
- What are the newest opportunities in the marketplace?

8:45–9:00 A.M.—Human Resources briefing: "What our internal customers are telling us."

- What are we doing to attract and retain the best and the brightest?
- What have recent surveys and exit interviews told us about sources of employee satisfaction and dissatisfaction?
- What are the most pressing human-resources issues today, and how are they likely to change in the immediate future?
- What is already being done to address these issues?

9:00–9:15 A.M.—Operations briefing: "What are the major operational/procedural issues confronting us today?"

- Operationally, what will we be doing differently tomorrow?
- How will new technologies in computer networks, production, engineering, manufacturing, or other technical systems affect the people in this room?
- What are these changes' most likely short-term and long-term effects?
- What can the people in this room do to help us realize the full benefits of the changes?

9:15–9:30 A.M.—Break.

Step 6: Conduct concurrent group discussions.

Divide the large group randomly into three smaller groups designated A, B, and C. Groups remain intact for a two-hour period, spending 40 minutes discussing each of the three topical briefings. The three briefing presenters rotate every 40 minutes among the groups. The purpose of these sessions is to answer questions the presentations may have raised, to discuss issues that team members wish to explore, and perhaps to make a recommendation or two for consideration by decision makers in the three areas. These sessions are highly interactive.

9:30–11:30 A.M.—Group discussions

Morning Group Assignments

	Internal Customers	External Customers	Operational Changes
Group A	9:30–10:10	10:10–10:50	10:50–11:30
Group B	10:10–10:50	10:50–11:30	9:30–10:10
Group C	10:50–11:30	9:30–10:10	10:10–10:50

11:30–noon—Summary of the morning.

Noon–1:00 P.M.—Lunch.

Step 7: Summarize the morning.

The three presenters each take five minutes to summarize the morning—what they heard in the three group sessions they conducted and what new directions will be considered by decision makers in those areas as a result. The rest of the time is open for comments by participants.

Step 8: Engage in creative problem-solving.

The afternoon session begins with a more playful activity but still focuses on the goals of the company. Its aim is to increase cohesiveness, tap into the creative powers of the groups, and possibly even to produce outcomes with significant dollar value to the company.

The A, B, and C groups designated in the morning remain intact for these activities. The three morning presenters are randomly assigned to one of the three groups. Each of the groups completes three projects. If you have more than eight people in a group, you may want to break them up into parallel groups doing the same activities. Here are some examples of problem-solving activities.

Project 1: Design a company Web page to be put on the Internet. What would the page look like? What other pages would you link it to? What would you do to make it appealing, dramatic, and professional? How will this page capture the essence of what we do and how we do it?

If your company already has a page on the Internet, focus the discussion on how it could be improved. The group discussion will be energizing; everyone in the group will learn more about the company and about their peers by listening to them. The discussion will bring out issues of corporate culture, vision, values, beliefs, customer service, and mission.

Project 2: Brainstorm possible new markets for our current products or services. Have fun; be as wild and creative as possible. Let your minds wander. Think about other industries and other uses. For example, there must be hundreds of problems a toilet plunger could solve other than the one for which it is purchased. There must be hundreds of ways you could modify existing products or hundreds of new uses for current products that

1:00–3:15 P.M.—Group Problem-Solving

Afternoon Group Assignments

	Design a Web Page	Brainstorm New Products/Markets	Plan Management Film Festival
Group A	1:00–1:45	1:45–2:30	2:30–2:45
Group B	1:45–2:30	2:30–3:15	1:00–1:45
Group C	2:30–3:15	1:00–1:45	1:45–2:30

3:15–3:30 P.M.—Break

3:30–3:50 P.M.—Spokesperson from Group A.

3:50–4:10 P.M.—Spokesperson from Group B.

4:10–4:30 P.M.—Spokesperson from Group C.

4:30–5:00 P.M.—Summary by team leader.

you have never considered. The specific group assignment is to create a list titled "The Top Ten Creative Ideas for Making Money with Our Current Product." Not only will this discussion be exciting for participants, it could conceivably produce a breakthrough product or way to sell an old product.

Project 3: Plan a "management movie festival." We all know that many training films are boring, sophomoric, and usually dated. In contrast, classic Hollywood movies are entertaining and sometimes have profound lessons; one example is the 1942 RKO film, *Pride of the Yankees.* What Hollywood movies would you choose for a training film library for our managers? The group assignment is to create a list titled "The Top Ten Movies That Teach Us How to Be Better Managers."

This discussion will be based on personal experience, recalling the movies participants believe have the greatest "message." Direct the discussion to what each message teaches about managing projects or leading people. Participants will develop a perspective of their peers they did not have prior to the discussion. In addition to group members learning more about each other, your company will gain a list of movies to show and discuss at future management retreats.

Step 9: Present creative solutions.

Each of the three groups elects a spokesperson to present the results of the group problem-solving sessions. The presentations from each group should be limited to a total of 15 minutes for all three products, with five minutes left for discussion.

Step 10: Summarize the day.

The leader should touch on the following themes:

- What do you think this day will do for you and the team?
- What were the high points of the day?
- What ideas in the afternoon session deserve further investigation?

How Do I Make One-Day Retreat Work for Me?

Assign someone the responsibility of policing the agenda.

Staying on track and on schedule requires a hard-nosed traffic cop. Consider giving your "timekeeper" a whistle and a special timer. When he or she says, "Time for the next session," all must move.

Sidebar conversations, one-on-one huddles, and extended opinion-sharing should be saved for breaks, lunch hour, or until the retreat is completed.

Select discussion topics and creative projects that specifically meet your needs.

The topics and assignments in our proposed agenda are merely suggestions. Appoint a committee to plan for the use of this tool in a way that meets the unique needs of your organization.

End the day with a reward.

Some of our clients end the day with a dinner and perhaps a humorous awards ceremony. Prizes are given to the groups that developed the most intriguing solutions to the afternoon assignments.

Don't wait for the "perfect" time to schedule the retreat.

You may never find a day that accommodates everyone's schedule. Pick a date far enough in advance so people can plan their calendars, and express your strong desire to see everyone there. Generally, the retreat works best following a major organizational effort—for instance, after tax season for an accounting firm, following the Christmas rush for a retail store, following a major ad campaign for an advertising firm.

7 TOOLS FOR YOU

Personal Vision

Resources needed:

None

Tools to consult:

Balance

What Problems Does Personal Vision Solve?

- This job is getting to me; how can I reduce the burden and the stress?
- I'm not sure I'm taking my life in the right direction.

What Is the Aim of This Tool?

The novelist Christopher Morley said, "There is only one success—to be able to spend life in your own way." The Roman senator Seneca said, "When a man does not know what harbor he is making for, no wind is the right wind."

Each one of us differs in that we have our own unique pattern of core values and beliefs. The quote by Christopher Morley means that the most effective and the happiest of people lead congruent lives—that is, they spend their days and exert their efforts in ways that are consistent with their unique core values and beliefs. As a result they experience less stress, less anxiety, and greater satisfaction with life.

Seneca's message is more straightforward. If you're going to be an effective person, worker, manager, executive, supervisor, parent, spouse, or friend, you need to plan your direction. In other, words you need a Personal Vision.

This tool helps you to examine your life to see whether you have congruence between your actions and your core values and beliefs. It defines the vision for your life in the same sense that Envision defined the vision for your company.

How Does Personal Vision Work?

Follow these steps to create your Personal Vision. Plan to take a minimum of several days to do a thorough job.

Step 1: Study the categories of beliefs, values, and desires.

The personal beliefs, values, and desires that you hold probably fall into some number of these categories. First go through the list and check off the categories where you expect most of your beliefs, values, and desires will fall.

___ Faith/religion/spirituality/worship
___ Spouse/significant other
___ Family/children/parents
___ Friends/relationships
___ Alliances/teamwork/partnerships
___ Finances/wealth/possessions
___ Health/fitness/energy
___ Hobbies/recreation/pleasure/relaxation
___ Achievement/creativity/career/work
___ Excellence/beauty/perfection/accuracy
___ Persistence/commitment/follow-through
___ Courage/risk taking/standing up for beliefs
___ Service/generosity/charity/sacrifice
___ Integrity/honesty/ethics/law
___ Learning/education/wisdom/intellect
___ Responsibility/reliability/loyalty
___ Leading/developing others/role modeling
___ Happiness/contentment/positive outlook
___ Forgiveness/acceptance/compassion

Step 2: Write your beliefs, values, and desires.

Look back at each category above; pay particular attention to the ones you checked off. Write down whatever personal beliefs, values, and desires are sparked by the categories. If you're like most people, you'll generate somewhere between 10 and 30 statements. Put the list away for a few days.

Step 3: Refine your list.

Take another look at your beliefs, values, and desires. Pare down the list by eliminating duplication and clustering those that are similar under a single statement.

Step 4: Prioritize your list.

Rank your beliefs, values, and desires with the most indispensable at the top of the list. You have created your Personal Vision. In Seneca's words, you now know what harbor you are steering for.

Step 5: Compare your list to your life.

Contrast your prioritized list—your "talk"—with how you actually spend your time and life—your "walk." Use the scale below to assess how much your daily behavior conforms to each item on the list.

5 : Almost fully 4 : Significantly 3 : Somewhat 2 : Partially 1 : Barely 0 : Not at all

What is the level of your scores overall? Do at least half of your items earn a 4 or 5? Where are your scores the highest—near the top of your list or near the bottom?

Step 6: Take steps to increase congruence.

What will you do to increase your scores overall and especially to increase the scores of items near the top of your list? Commit yourself to three behaviors that will increase congruence between your beliefs, values, and desires and the way you live your life, using the below.

Congruence-Creating Commitments

Commitment #1

Commitment #2

Commitment #3

How Do I Make Personal Vision Work for Me?

Here is a listing of core beliefs, values, and desires that someone might create for herself.

Sample Beliefs, Values, and Desires

- I love God and am here to serve Him.
- I seek inner peace and harmony.
- I value simplicity of life.
- I believe my life and the lives around me will be improved by maintaining a positive, optimistic, and noncritical outlook.
- I believe in strong family unity.
- I foster intellectual growth.
- I believe in the power and the need for daily prayer.
- I am honest in all things.
- I am a patient, understanding, and nurturing mother.
- I team with my spouse to raise happy children and support our parents in their final years.
- I am secure in what I do.
- I am efficient and detailed.
- I believe in the need to communicate persuasively, abundantly, and accurately.
- I remain physically fit.
- I like to exercise my imagination, creativity, and resourcefulness in my job.
- I seek to give my clients my best and to exceed their expectations.
- I believe in being a team player.
- I enjoy hard work.

How to Involve a Significant Other

If you are married or contemplating marriage or if you maintain a close personal relationship with someone, it is a good idea to involve that person in the Personal Vision process. But resist the temptation to do so until after you have created your own prioritized list of beliefs, values, and desires (Step 4). Work individually up to that stage. The ideal point to begin the discussion is at Step 5 or Step 6, depending on the nature of your relationship.

One great service you can provide to each other in Step 5 is to give each other feedback on your perception of the accuracy of each other's scores of attainment of your values and beliefs. In Step 6 you can help each other make commitments that will cause your relationship to flourish.

Sell It

Resources needed:

None

Tools to consult:

Change It

What Problems Does Sell It Solve?

- I need to improve my presentation and selling skills.
- How do I persuade my boss to go along with my ideas?
- How can I get other departments and my peers to be more cooperative?
- How can I get my employees to *want* to do what they *have* to do?
- How can I get people to change their behavior?

What Is the Aim of This Tool?

Leadership is a process of influence. As a manager you find yourself repeatedly in the position of convincing others to adopt a new way of thinking. Yet it's not easy to sell our ideas to others. Two factors especially make it difficult to get the agreement, acceptance, or behavior change we want. One is that people can be counted on to resist change. The other is that we sell ineffectively.

The major reason people resist change is because they are afraid that the change will cause them to give up something they cherish. Some of the outcomes they may dread are a loss of attention, control, freedom, predictability, preeminence, prestige, self-esteem, expertise, values, friendship, comfort, resources, or money. Sometimes this fear is so overwhelming and justified that there is little we can do to convince the owner of the fear that it won't be realized. Other times the fear can be dealt with, but we fail to take the steps necessary to do so.

Most of the mistakes we make when we try to convert other people over to our way of thinking probably fall into one of the "seven deadly sins of selling." Before you can be successful in presenting your ideas to others, you'll need to overcome these seven barriers.

The Seven Deadly Sins of Selling

1. We have too little belief in the value of what we're selling.
2. We have too little confidence that the prospect will want to buy what we're selling.
3. We know too little about the prospect's needs, pains, and desires.
4. We know too little about what we're selling.
5. We fail to realize why we're selling what we're selling.
6. We fail to ask for what we want in the right way.
7. We're neither emotionally nor intellectually prepared for the resistance of the prospect.

How Does Sell It Work?

People who consistently get others to agree with their ideas don't succeed by accident. They know what to do to encourage other people to want to cooperate with them. They take the steps described below and thereby avoid the "seven deadly sins of selling."

In the following steps we refer to the potential buyer of your ideas as the "prospect." This is not to imply a sales call in the customary context of selling a product, but merely to present a consistent short-hand way to identify the person you hope will embrace your ideas.

Step 1: Establish credibility.

Ideas don't sell as much as *people* sell. Be the kind of person from whom others will want to buy. Be known through your behavior as someone who makes reasonable requests, who cares for the welfare of others (the team, the company, and your boss), whose word can be trusted, and who follows through on commitments and fulfills promises.

Step 2: Generate rapport.

Make a connection with prospects. Create an appropriate psychological bond given your relationship with them and given the circumstances. Be pleasant and encouraging. Greet prospects with a warm smile and an upbeat "Hello." Call them by the name they like to be called. Make genuine inquiries about life situations important to them. Search for common passions to discuss. Listen more than you talk.

Step 3: Know exactly what you are asking for.

There are two vital outcomes of being sure you know what you want. First, you'll be able to state your proposal perfectly clearly and precisely to the prospect. Second, your clarity will build confidence in the prospect that you have thought your needs through. Ask yourself these questions about your request. What new behavior do I want? Am I sure that's what it is? What are my precise expectations of the prospect? If these expectations are met, will I be truly happy, or is there something else I'm looking for? Finally, what implications of fulfilling my request does the prospect need to understand in order to avoid buyer's remorse?

Step 4: Recognize* why *you are making this request.

What needs are you satisfying for yourself, for the other person, for your team, or for your company? Be honest about how much this request is for a personal need and how much it benefits others. What are your *personal* goals here? Is the request you plan to make the best way to achieve those goals, or should you ask for something other than this? (Notice that you don't need to consider the benefits of this request to others until Step 7, below.)

Step 5: Prepare to pay the price.

Most people don't think about what they need to pay for the cooperation of others, but there's usually a price. Consider the case of a manager who persuades an employee to assume a responsibility the manager once performed. A few examples of the possible costs to the manager of this cooperation are:

- Time spent training the employee on the new responsibility.

- Availability for coaching, counseling, and problem solving as the employee runs into snags.
- Giving appreciation of and recognition for the successes the employee achieves.
- Reduced performance in the area until the employee gets up to speed.
- Chagrin if the employee does the job better than the manager did.
- Authority and control relinquished to the employee along with the responsibility.
- Jealousy from other employees who may have felt *they* should have been given the responsibility.
- Expressions of concern from other supervisors who have no plans to delegate similar responsibilities to their employees.
- Disagreement by the manager's boss that this responsibility is appropriate to delegate.
- Loss of whatever personal fulfillment the manager previously received from carrying out the responsibility.
- An expected return of the favor by the employee.
- Using up a favor. (A manager can ask only so many major favors of the employee in a given time period.)

Be sure to identify the possible prices of getting what you ask for. Seeing a list as long as the one above might encourage you to change your request. Or you might choose to take steps in advance to reduce the costs.

Step 6: Ask for it—in the right way and at the right time.

Don't hint, wish, or wait for the other person to figure out what you want. Get to the point. Paint a vivid picture of what you want from the other person. Describe the behavior you desire. Believe you'll get a yes so that you ask convincingly. Ask at a time when the prospect will be listening to you and, if possible, positively predisposed toward cooperation with you. Finally, ask the right person—one who has the power to deliver.

Step 7: Demonstrate the benefits of cooperation.

The ultimate sales question is "What will cause a person to cooperate with you?" The ultimate answer to that question is "If the person believes that he or she stands to benefit in some way as a result of cooperating with you." In other words, the prospect will buy when he or she believes that the costs of buying are outweighed by the benefits. So the ultimate selling task is to demonstrate to prospects what they will gain by fulfilling your request. How do you do this? First by knowing the prospect—learning what's really important to him or her. What are the prospect's misgivings, concerns, worries, fears, embarrassments, and troubles? And what are the prospect's needs, desires, ambitions, goals, values, and beliefs? Think specifically about how your request helps the prospect to *avoid pain*—misgivings, concerns, worries, fears, embarrassments, and troubles. Think specifically how your request helps the prospect to *acquire pleasure*—fulfilling needs, desires, ambitions, goals, values, and beliefs. Make sure the prospect sees exactly how your idea contributes to pain avoidance and/or pleasure acquisition. To the extent possible, put even greater benefits to the prospect into your request than may be there right now.

Mastery of this step is the principal assurance of a successful sale. To achieve that mastery you need to know your prospect thoroughly. Listen at every opportunity so that you know the answers to two questions. Is pain avoidance or pleasure acquisition more important to that person right now? How can you show that your proposal eases one of those critical pains or brings one of those essential pleasures?

Step 8: Overcome objections.

What resistance to change will the prospect experience? What losses will he or she fear? As a result, what specific objections do you anticipate? When you know in advance what to expect, you can head off an objection by stating it yourself as an outcome of your request and then showing how your proposal resolves it. This impresses objectors with your honesty and sensitivity to their concerns. This also keeps you on the offensive—where you need to be in order to present, nondefensively, the resolution to the objection.

Whenever you receive an objection you did not anticipate, the strategy is a bit different. Follow these five steps.

1. *Listen* to the objection. Don't interrupt or counterattack.
2. *Repeat* the objection. Do this to make sure you've understood it. You'll also weaken the objection a bit when you give it back in the objector's own words.

3. *Validate* the objection and the objector. Say that you think it is a reasonable concern given the perspective taken by the objector and the information available to him or her up to the moment of your response.
4. *Test* the objection. Stated objections are often not the real McCoy. The objector may not be ready to be honest with you or may not even know why he or she is experiencing resistance to your idea. Test it by saying something like this: "Suppose I could show you that ________ would be taken care of. Would we then have a deal?" If the answer is yes, you know what you must do to ring up a sale. If the answer is no, the real objection has yet to be smoked out.
5. *Resolve* the objection. Once you know the true objection you can either offer the reasons why it isn't really of concern or state what you will do to ease the objector's concerns. If you can't do this, your idea won't fly.

How Do I Make Sell It Work for Me?

Armed with an understanding of the eight steps of selling, you are ready to use Sell It to market a specific idea to a specific person or group. Prepare yourself for that "sale" by writing your answers to the questions on the "Sell It Template" on pages 200–201. As you work in each box, refer to the descriptions of the eight selling steps for help in answering the questions.

Bear in mind the following points:

- Recognize the vital importance of the first step, "Establish credibility." If the prospect can't trust your motives or your honesty, little of what you do on the remaining steps will get you anywhere. Recognize that, unlike rapport, credibility with the prospect isn't something you can create on the spot or establish overnight. Credibility is a lot like a savings account. You add to it at every opportunity so that when in the future you need to draw on it, there will be enough of a balance to enable you to do what you want with the funds.
- Give prospects a thorough listening-to. Get to know them so well that you can show them how complying with your request will help them. As the great sales motivator Zig Ziglar once said, "No one ever lost a sale because he listened to the customer."

- Avoid the error of confusing features with benefits when selling your ideas. For example, don't sell your boss a new strategy for supervision of your employees; *do* sell your boss on a way to increase employee productivity.
- Avoid the error of selling an idea based on benefits to *you* rather than the benefits to the prospect. Don't sell a peer on your need for closer cooperation; *do* sell a peer on how she'll gain by cooperating more closely with you.
- Anticipate and count on receiving objections. See objections from the prospect as assets, rather than as liabilities. Remember that kites rise against, not with, the wind. Every objection you resolve successfully moves you closer to the sale.

Sell It Template

Name and title of prospect: ______________________________

Selling Step	Questions to Answer and Tasks to Perform
1. Establish credibility.	What particular credibility must you have with this prospect to sell this idea? ______________________________ ______________________________ ______________________________
2. Generate rapport.	What actions will you take at the meeting with this prospect to make a connection and create a psychological bond? ______________________________ ______________________________ ______________________________
3. Know exactly what you are asking for.	What do you want this person to do? What is the new condition you want to create as a result of your request? Be specific. Give quantities and dates as appropriate. ______________________________ ______________________________ ______________________________
4. Recognize why you are making this request.	What do you stand to gain personally from cooperation? Is asking for this particular behavior the best way to get it? ______________________________ ______________________________ ______________________________

5. Prepare to pay the price.	What might cooperation cost you? Are you willing to pay the price? Can anything be done to reduce it? __________ __________ __________
6. Ask for it—in the right way and at the right time.	Will you ask for the specific behavior you want and not merely hint at it? Are you sure you're asking the right person? What is the best timing for your request? How will you phrase the request? __________ __________ __________
7. Demonstrate the benefits of cooperation.	What have you done to get to know the pain this prospect wants to avoid and the pleasure this prospect wants to acquire? What are the primary benefits of cooperation to the prospect? __________ __________ __________
8. Overcome objections.	What objections do you expect? How will you resolve each one? __________ __________ __________

One-Finger Questions

Resources needed:

None

Tools to consult:

Lead with Your Ears
Gripe Session

What Problems Do One-Finger Questions Solve?

- I'm not getting constructive feedback from my boss.
- My managers and I are starving for some honest feedback from our employees.
- The members of our team aren't willing to say what we think of each other's performance.
- I don't believe we're hearing enough from our customers on how well we serve them.

What Is the Aim of This Tool?

Consider these scenarios:

- Kim, starved for performance feedback, musters the courage to walk into her supervisor's office to say, "Boss, how am I doing?" The supervisor looks up, and as though reading from a script, answers, "You're doing just fine, Kim. Don't worry—when you screw up, I'll tell you."
- A production supervisor caps off a performance appraisal meeting by asking, "So, Chris, what can I do to help you be more effective on the

job?" Without giving the question a second thought, Chris drones, "Nothing."

- A waiter returns to the table where he delivered entrées two minutes earlier to dutifully inquire, "How is everything?" Almost without fail he hears: "Fine."
- During a job interview the candidate is asked, "Is there anything about possibly working in this company in this job that concerns you?" The not-too-surprising answer from the prospect: "Not a thing."

Each of these scenarios demonstrates two realities of human communication. The first is that many people will not be honest about their reactions to your performance without encouragement. They may be afraid to hurt you; they may fear your response to an honest opinion; or they may not be accustomed to interpersonal candor. The second is that when you go on a fishing trip you usually return without a catch—especially if you don't use the right bait.

Had the four people just described used one-finger questions, their nets might have been full. One-Finger Questions encourage honesty, and the "bait" they offer is too good not to take.

How Do One-Finger Questions Work?

A One-Finger Question is a question that encourages a specific response. It cannot be answered with yes or no, and it can't easily be avoided.

Imagine that you're holding up your index finger and begin your question "What's the *one* . . . ?" Following this advice, the people in the four earlier scenarios would change their questions. Kim might ask, "Boss, if you had your choice of any one training program to send me to, what would it be?" The production supervisor might ask, "What's one thing I could change in my leadership behavior that would help you be more effective on the job?" The waiter would ask, "What's one thing I can do to make this meal a more enjoyable experience for you?" The interviewer might ask, "If you could think of one concern you might have about working here, what would it be?" Ask in this way to increase the probability of a valid, helpful response.

You increase the *probability* of a response because you give your listeners the option not whether to reply, but which among possible replies to choose. Another incentive to respond is that the listener is spared the necessity of composing an elaborate, carefully framed response.

You increase the *validity* of the answers you get because the minds of people thus queried are likely to fix on one of their most urgent concerns. One-Finger Questions also positively predispose people toward a helpful reaction. They give people choices, and people like choices. When you phrase your One-Finger Question as thoughtfully as those in the next section, you make it easy for listeners to give you a constructive and nonthreatening response, even when that response suggests that you need to change a part of your behavior.

How Do I Make One-Finger Questions Work for Me?

Here are seven groupings of One-Finger Questions you can use to get better information from others. Ask these questions or create your own. When you use a One Finger-Question it is usually helpful to put slight emphasis on the word "one." If your first question doesn't pull information from a reluctant subject, be persistent. In the first of the four earlier scenarios, Kim's boss might insist that she's doing fine and needs no training. Her response should be something like "I'm glad to hear that, but if there is *one* training program I might profit from, what would it be?"

To get feedback from your boss, ask questions like these:

- "What's one thing you would have liked me to do on that project that I didn't do?"
- "What's the best thing I can do to increase my value to you?"
- "What's one thing you would like to see more of [less of] in my service to you?"
- "If there is one training program you think I should attend, what is it?"
- "What one thing do I do that helps you the most [least]?"
- "What's the first thing I would need to change to become a more productive employee?"

To get feedback from your employees, ask questions like these:

- "What's one thing I can do to help you be a greater success?"
- "What's one behavior you'd like to see less of in me?"

- "What leadership behavior would you like to see more of in me?"
- "What one thing do I do that helps you the most [least]?"
- "If I set aside time each day to do one thing that I'm not doing, how would you suggest I spend that time?"
- "If I were to commit to changing one dimension of my leadership behavior, what dimension would you recommend for change?"
- "What's one thing we could have done to have kept you here?" (asked during an exit interview).

To get feedback from team members, ask questions like these:

- "If I were to do one thing that would make me a more useful member of this team, what would it be?"
- "What's one thing I can do to help you do your job better?"
- "What single team-player behavior would you like to see more of in me?"
- "What's one thing I can do to help reduce conflict on this team?"
- "What's one thing I can do less [more] to become a better team player?"
- "If six months from now you could look back and say that I had enhanced my contribution to this team more than any other member had, what one thing would it be that I had done to make that improvement?"

To get feedback from peers or other departments, ask questions like these:

- "What's one expectation you have of me that I fulfill less well than the others?"
- "What one thing do you think we need to do to work together better?"
- "If I did one thing to improve my service to you, what would you have that one thing be?"
- "What's your recommendation for one thing I can do to be more cooperative with you?"
- "On that last assignment we did together, what's one thing you wish I had done more [less] of?"
- "As we begin this new project, what one wish do you have for improvement over the way we've worked together in the past?"

To get feedback from customers, ask questions like these:

- "If you were to decide to change from us to a new supplier, what one most compelling factor would cause that change?"
- "What's one thing we can do, that we're not doing now, to give you the most exceptional service imaginable?"
- "On that last delivery, what one thing could we have done that we didn't do?"
- "What is the last dissatisfaction we created for you that you didn't tell us about?"
- "What's one way we can do it better next time?
- "What's one thing we can do more [less] of to give you greater value?"
- "What one thing could we have done to make this meal [shopping trip, service visit, etc.] a more enjoyable experience for you?"

To improve your interviews (selection, counseling, and data-collecting), ask questions like these:

- "What one question do you think I could have phrased differently to enable you to give a more helpful answer?"
- "If you were to add one additional comment to the answer you just gave, what would it be?"
- "What one question that I haven't yet asked should I ask?"
- "What one thing would you like to say that my questions thus far have not given you the opportunity to say?"
- "What one thing could I have done to make this a more productive interview?"
- "Let's assume for a minute that there's one concern you have about accepting a job with us [the behavior I'm describing, the way I'm going about collecting the data]. What is that one concern?"

To learn from participants in a training program how to improve it, ask questions like these:

- "The next time we offer this program, what one thing should we add to it [leave out]?"
- "What one important change should we make in this program before we offer it again?"
- "Which topic was most [least] helpful for you?"
- "What one thing should the instructor do differently the next time this program is offered?"

- "Who do you think is the ideal employee to benefit from this program?"
- "What's the first thing you're going to tell others about this program?"

Generating Feedback

Think of some people from whom you need more honest, constructive, and helpful feedback. Divide a sheet of paper into three columns: each person's name, what you need to learn, and the One-Finger Question you will use with each person. Then ask.

Person's Name	What I Want to Know	One-Finger Question

Lemons and Oranges

Resources needed:

Lemons and oranges or yellow and orange sticky dots

Tools to consult:

Full-Circle Growth
One-Finger Questions

What Problems Does Lemons and Oranges Solve?

- I'm not getting constructive feedback from my boss.
- My managers and I are starving for some honest feedback from our employees.
- The members of our team aren't willing to say what we think of each other's performance.

What Is the Aim of This Tool?

Someone once observed that we all exist as three persons: the "you" that you see; the "you" that others see, and the "you" that is. As a team leader, for example, you would have a definite perception of how well you praise the efforts of team members—the praise giver (you) that you see. At the same time, team members have a definite, and possibly different perception of your praising of them—the praise giver (you) that others see. Then there is your actual praising behavior—the praise giver (you) that is.

Of these three personae the one with least relevance is the third one, the "you" that is. It may be the one we most wish to understand, but it is the one least available to us. After all, who has the authority, in this life anyway, to claim knowledge of the real you?

So you are left with the "you" that you see and the "you" that others see as your only two sources of information about your performance. Do these two often different perceptions carry equal weight in revealing your behavior? Far from it! One of the two judgments really is a perception, but the other is a revelation of *reality*. To determine which of the two is reality, consider again your habits of praise. If on a scale of 0 to 5 team members rate your praising of them as 2 and you judge it as 4, which of the two numbers describes reality on that team? Of course it is the 2. This is how team members see you in your team leader role and has therefore become the basis on which they respond to you. The 2 has more influence on your success than the 4.

Do you want to know the reality of your leadership of others? Do you want to know how your boss views your performance? Do you want to know what your fellow team members think about your contribution to the team's goals? And do you want to learn these "realities" in a way that leads you directly to the appropriate responses to them?

Why Should I Use Lemons and Oranges Rather Than a Rating Scale?

Most feedback systems use quantitative rating scales like these.

5 : Almost always	5 : Strongly agree	4 : Completely
4 : Often	4 : Agree	3 : Mostly
3 : Sometimes	3 : Slightly agree	2 : Somewhat
2 : Infrequently	2 : Slightly disagree	1 : Partially
1 : Almost never	1 : Disagree	0 : Not at all
	0 : Strongly disagree	

If your goal is simply to evaluate and to document behavior, rating scales like these work well enough. If your goal is to encourage feedback recipients to improve performance, rating scales are woefully inadequate. Here's why.

1. A rater who is asked to label another person's behavior with either a number or a description feels like a judge. While a superior may feel comfortable rating a subordinate, it is

certainly difficult for most subordinates to rate superiors and for peers to rate each other. It is much less threatening to help a person identify priorities for improvement.

2. Raters of superiors will not want to have their scores attributed to them; they will almost certainly need to remain anonymous. In positive work climates, providers of Lemons and Oranges can be identified without fear of repercussion.
3. Numerical ratings are almost always summarized as averages. As a result, the richness of the individual responses is lost. For example, on the first five-point scale above a team leader of ten employees might receive an average score of 3.8 (close to "often"). That praise-giving score looks decent, doesn't it? But how would you feel, as the team leader, if you discovered that the 3.8 resulted from getting a top grade of 5 ("almost always") from six employees and a relatively poor grade of 2 ("infrequently") from the other four employees? Isn't this a result you need to act on in some way, rather than be lulled into a sense of security by the 3.8 average?
4. Our experience is that in rating superiors relatively few employees feel free to use the entire scale, often avoiding the lower extreme. Thus, in the example above those four scores of 2 may have been as harsh as the five employees were willing to be. They might really perceive a total absence of praise by the team leader.
5. What does a 4.0 mean? What does a 3.5 mean? Who's to say? By contrast, when 40 percent of your staff chooses to give you a lemon—as might have happened in the example above—you have come face to face with a priority area for leadership development.
6. There is a temptation for some recipients to compare their scores to those of their peers, rather than focus on the meaning of the scores themselves. Comparisons among managers are less meaningful with Lemons and Oranges, so recipients of feedback are encouraged to focus solely on their own data.

How Does Lemons and Oranges Work?

The purpose of Lemons and Oranges is to get honest and nonthreatening feedback in a fashion that points you clearly in the direction you need to go to respond positively. (See *Full-Circle Growth* for a detailed response strategy.)

The steps below are based on applying this tool to the relationship you have with those who report to you, but it can be generalized to many different interpersonal contexts. It will be immediately apparent how you can also use Lemons and Oranges with peers, superiors, customers, family members, or any other group.

Step 1: Make your list of behaviors.

Construct a list of 20 or so supportive leadership behaviors employees should expect to see in you. Better yet, ask them to construct a list of the 20 needs they have of you for great leadership. Put each one on a sheet of paper numbered from 1 to 20, or however many behaviors you generate.

Step 2: Buy and bag the fruit.

Purchase three lemons and three oranges for every person who reports to you. Place each set of three lemons and three oranges in a paper bag along with a dark felt-tip permanent marker. Staple a leadership list to each bag of fruit. (If you have more than 25 items on your list, add one lemon and one orange for every 5 to 10 items over the first 20. Avoid exceeding 35 items on any one list.)

Note that you're not limited to using fruit for this exercise. You could use orange and yellow sticky dots. You might ask employees to assign three Ts (for "top") and three Bs (for "bottom") to the list of numbered leadership expectations. You might also ask them to circle three of the smiling and three of the frowning faces placed in front of each item on the list.

Step 3: Pass out the fruit.

Give each employee a bag along with instructions to place numbers on the three oranges corresponding to the three leadership behaviors that you display *more* consistently than the other 17. Have them place numbers on the three lemons corresponding to the three leadership behaviors you display *less* consistently than the other 17. Do the exercise yourself as well.

An important consideration at this point is anonymity. Decide what's best for your organization. In some work climates employees would be paralyzed at the thought of being identified with their upward feedback. In many others this would not be a problem. Since all employees must give you three lemons and three oranges—no more, no less—no one should feel threatened, even if you ask them to put their initials on the paper bag. All they're doing is helping you identify which three behaviors are at the top of your list and which are at the bottom. Everyone has three at the top and three at the bottom, even the best of leaders.

Step 4: Collect the fruit.

After employees do their job, dump the fruit on your desk to see what you have. Examine the results, looking for consensus opinions. What do clusters of lemons or clusters of oranges at one item say about the impact of your leadership behavior? What does any apparent randomness in the ratings say about the varied needs of your direct subordinates or about possible inconsistent treatment you may subject them to? How do your perceptions of yourself compare to the perceptions of your team's "reality"? What additional information do you need from them to gain maximum value from giving the feedback?

Step 5: Reveal what you learned.

Meet with employees to thank them for their help. It would be good for them to hear you comment on what you learned and how you plan to change your leadership style as a result. If you need additional information, ask for it, but be careful not to place employees in a compromising or threatening position. For any feedback that surprises you, say something like this: "I was jolted to get four lemons as a listener. That tells me you're seeing something in my behavior that I'm blind to. What is it that I'm not aware of? Please tell me what behavior you see that tells you I don't listen well." Respond thankfully and cordially to their answers. This is also a great opportunity to use *One-Finger Questions.*

Step 6: Reveal what you're going to do.

Make commitments for specific changes in your leadership behavior in response to the feedback. Ask employees for whatever specific help they can give you to make the changes. Do this when you meet with them, if possible, or after you've taken whatever additional time you need.

Step 7: Find out how well you're doing.

Meet with employees again in three months for face-to-face input on how well you're fulfilling your commitments. Continue to improve your leadership and reap the resulting employee performance dividends.

How Do I Make Lemons and Oranges Work for Me?

Three different inventories appear below that you might use as a starting point in building a list you can use to request Lemons and Oranges from superiors, from subordinates, and from peers. Feel free to add to or subtract from the list or reword the items to make them more relevant to your situation.

Inventories of Sample Lemons and Oranges List Items

Superiors giving feedback to subordinates

1. Gets work done on time, under budget, and to specifications.
2. Pays thorough attention to detail; produces high-quality work.
3. Works with enthusiasm, energy, and a positive mental attitude.
4. Treats customers warmly, responsively, and professionally.
5. Makes suggestions for better, faster, and less costly procedures.
6. Engages in continuous improvement in own processes.
7. Is honest and trustworthy.
8. Works to full potential.
9. Is creative and innovative in ways that generate increased income.
10. Continues to grow and improve his/her skills.
11. Works effectively with little or no direct supervision.
12. Remains accountable for his/her actions and the results of his/her work.
13. Strives to help peers succeed; is a team player.
14. Sees that most problems are solved before they come to the boss's attention.
15. Keeps the boss informed; is a reliable source of both good news and bad news.

Subordinates giving feedback to superiors

1. Strives toward a definite vision and purposeful set of desired outcomes for our unit. Knows where he/she is going.
2. Translates his/her vision into terms we can grasp, identify with, and be inspired by. Makes us a part of the vision.

3. States clear expectations for our performance so we know exactly what is required and how we are to provide it.
4. Appraises/evaluates employee performance regularly and fairly. Lets us know where we stand.
5. Constructively criticizes unmet expectations and poor effort. Imposes consequences on those who subvert team effort.
6. Recognizes fulfilled expectations and hard work. Praises and rewards contributors to a team effort. Makes us feel appreciated.
7. Listens. Is open to the ideas and suggestions of others.
8. Coaches, mentors, and trains. Gives us the knowledge and skills we need to be effective.
9. Backs us up and supports us when, despite our best efforts, we fail. Tolerates well-intentioned mistakes.
10. Models a seriousness of purpose. Expects each one of us to give our best to the team effort.
11. Makes work enjoyable. Encourages a healthy balance between our work and our personal lives.
12. Makes decisions when needed. Is assertive and is willing to take risks.
13. Shares the limelight. Gives credit to others for their contributions.
14. Resolves conflict with others and between others tactfully, directly, and decisively.
15. Delegates both responsibility and authority. Shares power with us.

Giving feedback to peers

1. Embraces the vision of the team—its direction, aspirations, and core values.
2. Shows that he/she values the mission and goals of the team at least as highly as his/her own personal goals.
3. Cooperates with colleagues; pitches in to help them when they need it. Does not engage in destructive competition with other team members.
4. Keeps colleagues informed; sees that they have the quality and quantity of information that they need on time in order to do their jobs.
5. Coaches, mentors, and trains colleagues who stand to benefit from his/her knowledge, skills, and experience. Responds positively when colleagues request advice or help.
6. Remains accountable to team members for fulfilling their expectations. Accepts full responsibility for assignments and their outcomes. Follows through on promises and responds to requests from team members. Remains committed to doing a good job. Gives his/her best to the team effort.

7. Continually makes suggestions for doing things better, faster, less expensively, and more creatively; speaks up with ideas for improvement.
8. Is honest and trustworthy; won't misrepresent feelings or the facts about any issue. Admits to mistakes; corrects them quickly and willingly.
9. Defends and supports colleagues at every opportunity.
10. When the need arises to criticize a colleague, does so constructively and forthrightly, taking great care to do it in private and to condemn the deed and not the doer.
11. Praises, recognizes, and thanks colleagues liberally. Is their cheerleader. Shares the limelight with them. Gives credit to them for their contributions.
12. Is his/her toughest critic; remains aware of and sensitive to the impact he/she has on colleagues. Asks for appraisals of performance; responds well to the feedback received.
13. Listens to the ideas of others. Remains open to their ideas and suggestions. Remains flexible and ready to consider new behaviors. Is willing to step out of own comfort zone.
14. Tolerates the well-intentioned mistakes of colleagues; encourages them in times of failure. Remains patient, forgiving, and emotionally in control.
15. Maintains a positive mental attitude. Remains optimistic, enthusiastic, and energetic.

Frame It

Resources needed:

Picture frame diagram

Tools to consult:

Sell It
Fight Right
Balance

What Problems Does Frame It Solve?

- There's a person I'm having a lot of trouble dealing with.
- How do I gain control of my emotions when dealing with difficult people?

What Is the Aim of This Tool?

The greatest barrier to maintaining effective relationships with others is our failure to step outside our own skins to see what's really going on. Like an uncontrollable drunk at a party, we are oblivious to the impact our behavior has on others. At the same time, we often don't make the effort to understand why the other person is behaving in a way that has us so upset.

People with the ability to "frame" an issue can step back and view it from a detached, analytical perspective. They are often said to have great "people" skills. They have this uncanny knack of remaining calm and helpful even in the midst of the most heated arguments. When verbally attacked by others they appear to rise into their heads in order to respond thoughtfully instead of dropping into their stomachs to react viscerally.

The more analytical and dispassionate you are when you deal with a difficult person and when you express your disagreement, the more successful you will be. When you are overtaken by your emotions, you lose your ability to think and to act rationally. You are more likely to attribute devious motives and intent to the other person and less likely to seek to understand the forces causing the troublesome behavior. You become victim to distortion and acrimony; the other person becomes victim to your vindictiveness.

Frame It frees you from the bondage of self-centeredness in times of disagreement and interpersonal conflict. You'll learn how to step outside your own skin. You'll become a detached observer of your confrontations with others. You'll gain insights into becoming a part of the solution rather than half or more of the problem.

Here are a few instances to which you can apply Frame It.

- Your boss threatens you, criticizes you harshly, or won't take action on an urgent situation you've uncovered.
- A peer demeans you in front of others, spreads vicious rumors about you, or stabs you in the back.
- An employee is insubordinate, blows up in a coaching session, or is overwhelmed by a defeatist attitude.
- A customer demands VIP treatment, lies to you, or bitterly complains about your service.
- You have an argument or a disagreement with someone.

How Does Frame It Work?

Frame It uses a picture-frame diagram, as shown on page 218, to help you analyze difficult encounters. First, you are asked to look at the "picture" inside the frame to describe exactly what you saw the other person do or heard the person say. You make no interpretations, judgments, or presumptions. Second, you use each of the four segments of the frame around the picture to understand *why* you saw or heard what you did.

The segments of the frame

Top segment: "Pain/Frustration." People who are mean, rude, ugly, and nasty to you are often that way because of some pain they feel. That pain may be ten years old, ten months old, ten weeks old, ten days old, or ten seconds old. It may be embedded in your experience with the person, or it may have nothing to do with your relationship. Many of us react to pain and frustration by lashing out at those around us.

Right segment: "Fear/Insecurity." Fear operates much like pain. One of the outcomes of fear is anger. Insecure people often cover up their lack of confidence by acting out toward others in negative ways.

Left segment: "Hopelessness/Despair." When life creates a feeling of desperation, when people become disheartened, or when they feel that they've lost control in their lives, some retreat into a shell of depression. Others get angry with the world and verbally abuse those who try their compromised patience.

Bottom segment: "Interpersonal Incompetence." There's a saying that goes "Never attribute to malice that which can be

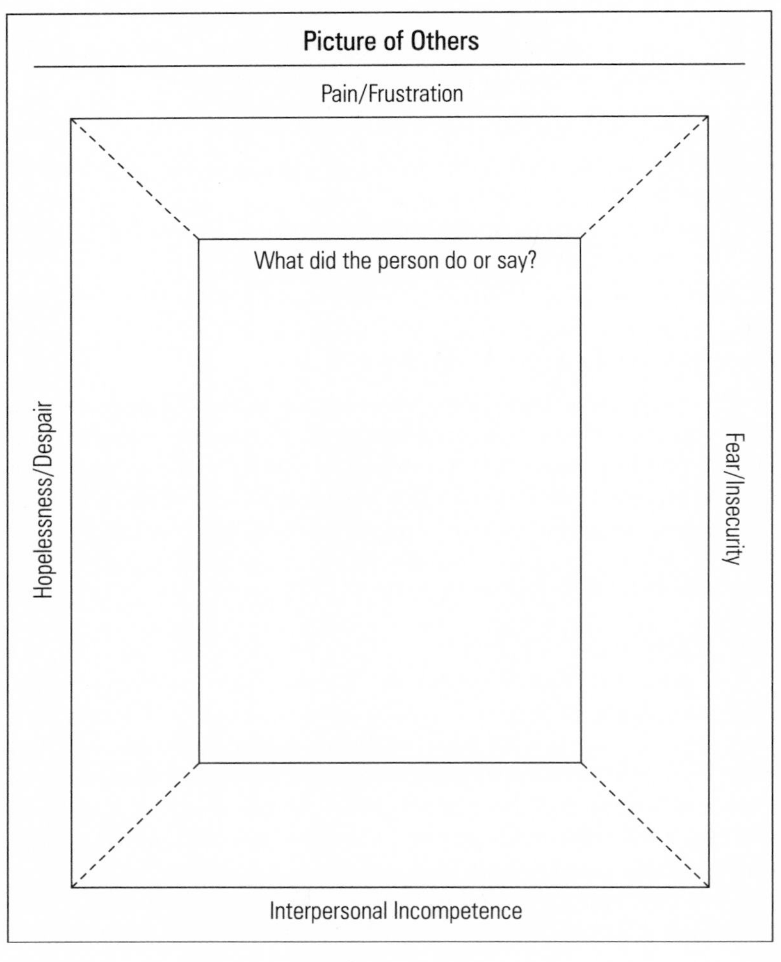

explained by incompetence." The corollary is "Give people credit for their stupidity." There are many interpersonally incompetent people out there. When things go wrong for them or when they are challenged, they simply don't have any constructive responses at their disposal. They didn't learn any at home, at school, on the streets, at seminars, or out of books.

Now that you understand the idea of Frame It, you're ready to use the steps to gain new insights into your dealings with the challenging people in your life. Frame It won't necessarily give you a guaranteed solution to the interpersonal dilemmas you face, but it will give you a clear picture of what's really going on. You can then use your decision-making skills, now free of bias, to fix the problem.

Step 1: Complete the "Picture of Others."

In the center of the picture-frame diagram labeled "Picture of Others," write your response to the question, What did the person do or say? If the event had been recorded on videotape, what would we see and hear? If you must rely on what another person *claimed* was done or said, note that on the picture.

Step 2: Fill in the four segments of the frame.

To what extent is this person acting out of pain, fear, hopelessness, or interpersonal incompetence? Fill in as many of the four sides with your analysis as possible. You may be tempted to conclude that none of these are relevant and that the person is just plain nasty. (We're onto you!) Fight that temptation. Write at least one statement in each segment of the frame. Guess if you have to.

Step 3: Tuck the frame away.

Put the frame out of sight for at least 24 hours. When you see it again, study what you wrote on it. Underline the entries that you're convinced are the truth. Add whatever other insights into the other person's behavior that you have.

Step 4: Study the picture and the frame.

Does the analysis on the frame help you understand this person's behavior? If it does not, you may not yet have uncovered all the frame factors operating in the situation. Put the frame away for another 24-hour period before you continue with the analysis. If the information on the frame appears to be useful, exactly how does it help you? Does it make you feel less emotional about the behavior? Does it give you any ideas on how to deal with the behavior more effectively or how to get the person interested in changing it? (See *Sell It.*)

Step 5: Complete the "Picture of Self."

If the situation you're analyzing is an argument, a disagreement, or any situation where the two of you have exchanged heated words or acted out against each other, you must examine your own frame. What did *you* do or say? If the event had been recorded on videotape what would we see and hear? Use the picture-frame diagram labeled "Picture of Self" on the following page to analyze your response.

Step 6: Fill in the four sides of the frame.

To what extent were you acting out of pain, fear, hopelessness, or interpersonal incompetence? Fill in as many of the four sides as possible.

Step 7: Study the picture and the frame.

Does the analysis on the frame help you understand your behavior? If it doesn't, you may not yet have uncovered all of the frame factors operating in the situation. If it does, how has this analysis helped you? Does it make you feel less emotional about the situation? Does it give you any ideas on how to improve your relationship with the person?

How Do I Make Frame It Work for Me?

- After going through the steps of Frame It, you should be in a better position to bring about positive change in your relationship with this person. You'll be encouraged to place less blame on the person and will be more ready to engage in mutual problem solving with the help of a tool like *Fight Right.*
- Don't show other people the frames you construct of their behavior. You can imagine the destructiveness that might accompany such a revelation.
- One great way to use this tool is for each person in a disagreement to complete a frame on his or her own behavior (Steps 5 and 6) without necessarily doing one on each other. The subsequent discussion, in which each accepts responsibility for his or

her behavior, will go a long way toward bringing about a constructive resolution.

- Do not misunderstand the purpose of Frame It. It is not intended to justify or to excuse improper behavior. It is intended to give you more control. By calmly analyzing the causes of another person's behavior, you free yourself from the knee-jerk reaction that often triggers emotional suffering. Instead, you position yourself to insist upon more appropriate behavior.

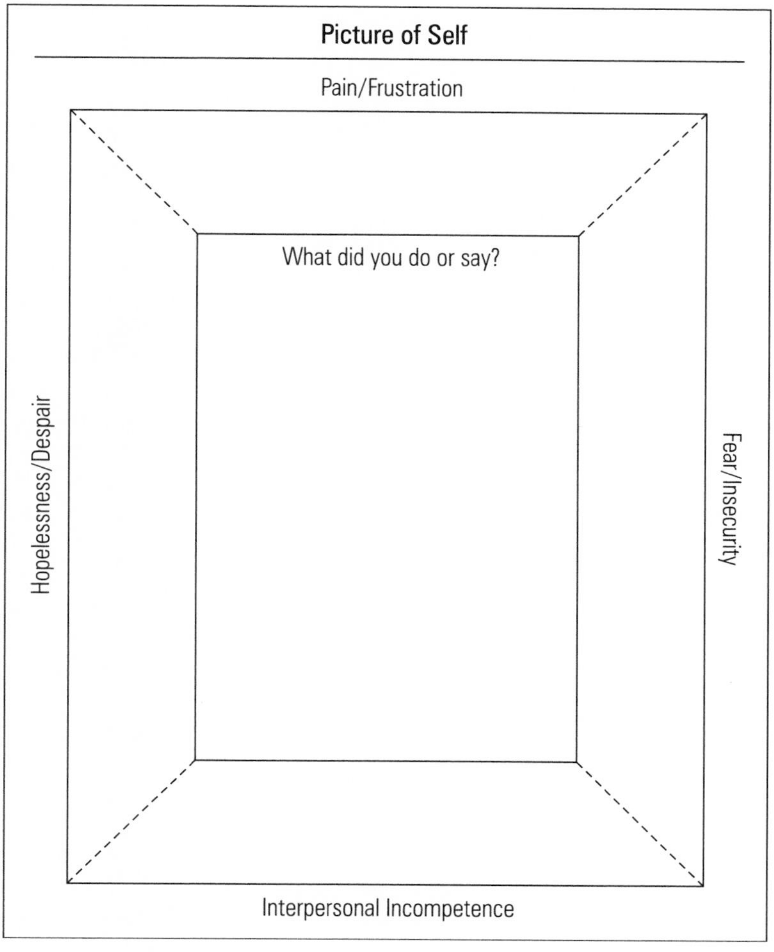

Balance

Resources needed:

None

Tools to consult:

Personal Vision

What Problems Does Balance Solve?

- I'm not balancing the needs of my personal and professional responsibilities. What do I do?
- How do I coach an employee who is having trouble balancing home with work?
- This job is getting to me; how can I reduce the burden and the stress?

What Is the Aim of This Tool?

If we have both careers and families, we have tough choices. Do we attend our daughter's soccer game or put finishing touches on the new sales proposal? Do we visit Mom in the nursing home or stay late at the office learning that new computer program? Do we leave the office early and work out in the gym or spend another hour on the Internet checking out the competition? What do I take to the beach, my laptop or a good book?

When our lives are in equilibrium we find ways to make our customers and our families happy. We find ways to balance the expectations at work with the expectations at home. And finally we realize that even though we can't be all things to all people we can be all things to the right people.

The purpose of this tool is to help you find balance in your life so that when you retire you will have something to retire to. A corollary purpose is help your team members achieve balance in their lives. Once they see you walk the talk about balance you will improve working conditions for all. Remember, it's tough to get employees to perform if they have bleeding ulcers, experience coronary attacks, or suffer from chronic depression.

How Does Balance Work?

Balance is a systematic, structured method for assessing the relative commitment and energy you devote to your personal life versus your professional life. This assessment leads to a series of steps for restoring equilibrium.

Step 1: Complete the "Balance Questionnaire."

This questionnaire on page 224, contains eleven descriptions of ways of treating and behaving toward others. Rate how you think your family and your coworkers see you in terms of these behaviors. Don't rate how well *you think* you engage in them.

Step 2: Add the scores in the two columns.

Which of your two scores is higher? Are you comfortable with the difference between them? Do you think they reflect a life that is in balance?

The bottom line of your scores is this: Are *you* happy with them? Don't let anyone else tell you what a balanced life is. If you accept these scores as being about right, there's no reason to change. If you believe you need to take action to restore balance in your home/work life, continue on to Step 3.

Step 3: Let coworkers and family members score your questionnaire.

Ask the people whom you had in mind as you completed the questionnaire fill it out themselves. How do their scores compare to yours? Do their scores reflect a life more, or less, out of balance than you originally thought?

Step 4: Develop action plans.

If your family score is low in relation to your coworker score, consider these options:

- Become more determined to plan your workday so that you don't have to take work home.

Balance Questionnaire

Use this scale for your assessment of how often family members and coworkers would say they see you do the behavior.

0 : *Never* 1 : *Rarely* 2 : *Infrequently* 3 : *Sometimes* 4 : *Often* 5 : *Almost always*

Behavior Toward Others in the Past 12 Months	Rating from Family Members	Rating from Coworkers
1. I listen to what they have to say.	______	______
2. I treat them with sensitivity and thoughtfulness.	______	______
3. I devote psychic energy when I am around them—I am plugged in and attentive.	______	______
4. I work at improving the quality of our relationship.	______	______
5. I show concern for their needs and problems.	______	______
6. I coach and counsel them.	______	______
7. I talk about our mutual goals.	______	______
8. I confide in them; I share my innermost feelings.	______	______
9. I spend time with them.	______	______
10. I compliment them.	______	______
11. They can count on me; I fulfill my promises.	______	______
TOTAL SCORE	______	______

- Commit to family retreats, vacations, and events. Hold them sacrosanct.
- Reconnect with your spiritual side.
- Negotiate assignments with your boss so that your workload becomes more manageable.
- Delegate more responsibilities to others who are available to help you, but be careful not to throw *their* lives out of balance.
- Talk to a career counselor.
- Talk to a family counselor.
- Consider switching to a less demanding, and possibly less financially rewarding, career.

If your coworker score is low in relation to your family score, consider these options:

- If it isn't broke, don't fix it; continue to hold your family above your work.
- Talk to a career counselor.
- Consider switching to a more motivating job or career.
- Seek more creative work assignments within your current position.
- Seek training that may make you a more responsive manager.

How Do I Make Balance Work for Me?

Talk about your scores with family members.

Your family has a vested interest in your scores. Share the questionnaire with them. The simple act of discussing the scores is a powerful first step toward achieving balance in your life through a personal action plan that your family can support.

The discussion may also bridge misperceptions. For example, they may have scored you higher—or lower—than you thought they would. The questionnaire provides a basis for exploring feelings, perceptions, and values that have been implicit for too long. Bring them out in the open where they can be dealt with.

Talk about your scores with someone at work.

Talking about the scores with a colleague may also be part of your action plan. Just as family members have a vested interest in your scores, so too will colleagues. You may want to show it to your boss, a member of your board of directors (if you're the boss), a trusted peer, or someone in the human resources department. Ask the person(s) you choose to rate you independently in the "co-worker column," if they have not already done so. Discuss the reasons for whatever differences exist in your scores. The people who help you with this might even ask you to return the favor by discussing the scores they give themselves on the questionnaire.

Use your scores to negotiate new role expectations.

You can use the assessment as a starting point in discussions with your family and professional colleagues. Tell them what you discovered and what you'd like to change. Start talking about mutual expectations. What should they expect from you and why? What should you expect from them and why? What short-term and long-term consequences can you both expect once you begin to bring your life into balance?

Use the assessment as the basis for employee training, counseling, and coaching.

Although we recommend that the results of the questionnaire be private and confidential, the data could be used for one-on-one coaching and counseling. Ask team members to complete the questionnaire as part of periodic performance evaluations. Use the tool to help employees develop personal action plans for balancing the demands of home and work.

Ask your spouse to use this tool if he or she also has a career.

Compare your results and support each other in whatever action plans the two of you devise.

Revisit the questionnaire every year.

Our lives are in constant flux. Your scores today may be different from those next month or the month after that. Use this tool for a yearly "balance" checkup.

Action Index

This Action Index is your path to the power tools you need. Here's how we suggest you proceed. First, go through this entire index. Read the problems solved by the tools within each of the five focus areas. Once you've surveyed the problem statements, place a single check (✔) in front of the statements that mildly interest you. These checks indicate the tools you'll want to read when you can get to them. Next, place a double check (✔✔) in front of the statements that *vitally* interest you. These statements lead you to the tools you want to read right now!

Leadership problems

Problem	Power Tools	Page
___ Our managers have tunnel vision. How can I get them to focus on the strategic forces affecting our future?	*Vista* *Envision* *Strategic Planner*	30 24 35
___ Not enough people are following my lead.	*Great Expectations* *Culture Print*	49 16
___ Too many people around here don't have the same priorities I do.	*Culture Print* *Tactical Planner* *Strategic Planner* *Lead with Your Ears*	16 40 35 54

Teamwork problems

Problem	Power Tools	Page
___ We have an important task ahead that we won't achieve unless we all work together as a unit.	*Team Builder* *Meeting Leader*	60 72
___ We're not all marching to the same beat. Sometimes it feels like we're not even all part of the same band.	*Team Builder* *Culture Print* *Envision* *Strategic Planner*	60 16 24 35
___ We need more teamwork in this company—from top to bottom.	*Team Links* *Team Builder* *Players On the Bench* *One-Day Retreat*	67 60 79 178
___ Team members aren't on the same wavelength; they don't mesh as they should.	*Team Builder* *One-Day Retreat*	60 178
___ I need to improve my conflict resolution skills.	*Fight Right* *Frame It*	84 216
___ There's too much conflict and bickering around here.	*Fight Right*	84
___ I'm not satisfied with my ability to run effective meetings.	*Meeting Leader* *Team Builder*	72 60

Motivation problems

Problem	Power Tools	Page
___ The new people we hire are diluting the culture we've worked so hard to create.	*Culture Print*	16
___ Employees claim, "We don't get paid our fair share, given the money this company makes."	*Salary 101* *Performance Pay*	108 113
___ How can I make our employees more cost-conscious?	*Salary 101*	108
___ My employees aren't taking responsibility for their personal development.	*Brown Bag*	123
___ How do I recognize our support staff and our unsung heroes?	*Players On the Bench* *Hero Table* *Home Links*	79 96 119
___ I'm a praise miser.	*Hero Table*	96
___ Our people have a great deal of pent-up anger and hostility. How can we vent it constructively and move forward as a team?	*Gripe Session* *Aftermath*	156 128
___ We've just had a major downsizing. What can I do to start building the team again?	*Aftermath* *Gripe Session* *Tactical Planner* *Team Builder* *One-Day Retreat*	128 156 40 60 178
___ Our performance reviews don't work; managers hate giving them and employees hate receiving them.	*Appraise for Success* *Full-Circle Growth*	101 161
___ I want to tie pay to performance in such a way that people are motivated to improve their performance and enhance the bottom line.	*Appraise for Success* *Salary 101* *Performance Pay*	101 108 113

	Problem	Power Tools	Page
___	We need to do a better job of developing our people.	*Appraise for Success*	101
		Brown Bag	123
		Performance Fixer	172
		Criticism Template	144
		Full-Circle Growth	161
___	We need to know the latest in management development but don't have time for off-site training.	*Brown Bag*	123
___	How can we get greater impact from the training we do?	*Brown Bag*	123
		Culture Print	16
___	We need to find ways to make sure the families of our employees don't feel neglected and abused because of our workload.	*Home Links*	119
		Balance	222
___	We want our employees to get maximum support from home.	*Home Links*	119

Growth problems

	Problem	Power Tools	Page
___	We need to figure out better ways of doing things around here.	*One-Day Retreat*	178
		Change It	151
		Tactical Planner	40
		Strategic Planner	35
		Lead with Your Ears	54
___	The next time I implement change, how do I do a better job of introducing it than the last time?	*Change It*	151
		Tactical Planner	40
___	I have a problem performer on my hands.	*Great Expectations*	49
		Performance Fixer	172
		Frame It	216
		Fight Right	84
		Criticism Template	144
		Sell It	193

Your problems

Problem	Power Tools	Page
___ How do I persuade my boss to go along with my ideas?	*Sell It*	193
___ I'm not getting constructive feedback from my boss.	*One-Finger Questions*	202
	Lemons and Oranges	208
	Full-Circle Growth	161
___ I am uncomfortable giving criticism to others.	*Criticism Template*	144
___ If my employees were honest, they might tell me I'm not a good listener.	*Lemons and Oranges*	208
	One-Finger Questions	202
	Lead with Your Ears	54
___ How do I gain control of my emotions when dealing with difficult people?	*Frame It*	216
	Fight Right	84
___ I'm turning into a pessimist.	*Whiner Cup*	90
	Personal Vision	188
___ I'm not balancing the needs of my professional and personal responsibilities. What do I do?	*Balance*	222
	Personal Vision	188
___ How do I coach an employee who is having trouble balancing home with work?	*Balance*	222
	Personal Vision	188
___ I'm not sure I'm taking my life in the right direction.	*Personal Vision*	188
___ This job is getting to me; how can I reduce the burden and the stress?	*Personal Vision*	188
	Balance	222
	Fight Right	84
	Frame It	216
___ There's a person I'm having a lot of trouble dealing with.	*Frame It*	216
	Fight Right	84
	Performance Fixer	172

Do You Need Help with Your Power Tools?

Sam Deep and Lyle Sussman can show you how to get the greatest value from the Power Tools. Even though many of the tools are "do-it-yourself," Sam and Lyle are often called on to perform these six "tool-sharpening" services.

- Diagnose the need for specific tools in particular corporate settings.
- Conduct Power Tool Retreats where executives learn how to use the tools in their company.
- Provide midcourse correction to Power Tool applications already under way.
- Oversee the application of those tools that will benefit from outside facilitation.
- Introduce you to several Power Tools not published in this book.
- Invent customized tools to solve your unique management problems in areas such as team building, conflict resolution, and communication.

The authors also provide keynote presentations, leadership training, and corporate consulting services on a wide range of business topics.

To bring Sam Deep or Lyle Sussman to your company call 1-800-526-5869. Direct e-mail requests to deepsam@aol.com. Mail inquiries to:

Sam Deep
1920 Woodside Road
Glenshaw, PA 15116

About the Authors

Sam Deep is a motivational speaker, management trainer, and organizational consultant. He formerly served as an academic administrator at the University of Pittsburgh, where he also taught in the communication department.

Lyle Sussman is professor of management in the School of Business, University of Louisville, Kentucky. He has a doctorate from Purdue University in communications and industrial relations. He serves on the faculties of several state and national banking schools.

Deep and Sussman give speeches, conduct seminars, and perform consulting for a variety of organizations such as *Fortune* 500 companies, health-care organizations, public school systems, colleges and universities, professional associations, and government agencies. Recent clients include Alcoa, American Bankers Association, Austrian National Bank, Bahamas Ministry of Tourism, Bayer, Blockbuster Video, Brown Williamson, Carnegie Mellon University, Dean Witter, Deloitte & Touche, General Electric, Hallmark Cards, Humana, KFC, Ketchum Communications, Kraft Food Service, Mellon Bank, Merck, National Cattleman's Association, PPG Industries, Pittsburgh Symphony, Presbyterian University Hospital, Puerto Rico Hotel and Tourism Association, Rally's, Rockwell International, Southwestern Bell, Union Switch & Signal, U.S. Postal Service, Veterans Administration, Westinghouse, and Xerox.

Deep and Sussman's ideas about management have been featured in articles in the *Chicago Tribune, Cosmopolitan, Self, USAir Magazine, Working Woman, Boardroom Reports,* and *Executive Report,* to name a few. Their last four taped programs have been shown on USAir's Inflight Audio Entertainment. The authors have been interviewed on countless radio and television stations, including WGN (Chicago) and CNN-FN. Their management columns have appeared in four newspapers. As best-selling authors they have over one million books in print in more than a dozen languages.